"In *What Lights You Up?* Mary Olson-Menzel *provides essential tools for navigating today's job market with confidence and clarity. Her practical advice ensures that you're not just choosing a job, but a career that genuinely excites and motivates you.*

—Morag Barrett,
Keynote Speaker, Executive Coach, Leadership Facilitator,
author, and CEO of Skyeteam

"Whatever your age or professional journey, *What Lights You Up?* is the handbook for your favorite career future. This book is a must-read for anyone who wants to identify their unique attributes for bigger success."

—Michael Clinton,
Former President and Publishing Director of Hearst Magazines and
author of ROAR *Into the Second Half of Life!*

"*What Lights You Up?* is a masterclass in career transformation, showcasing Mary Olson-Menzel's deep expertise and long-standing commitment to personal and professional development. With over 25 years of experience, Mary coaches clients to recognize and harness their 'inner light,' offering not just a book but a powerful toolkit for anyone seeking to elevate their career. Her unique MVP 360 Pivot Program, distilled within these pages, provides practical exercises and insights that guide readers to uncover what truly motivates them and how to leverage these passions in the workplace. This work is a testament to Mary's profound understanding of the job market's evolving dynamics and the critical role of individuality in achieving professional success. It is an essential resource for anyone ready to enhance their career path with authenticity and purpose."

—Camille Burns,
CEO of Women Presidents' Organization

"This book illuminates the path to a fulfilling career with actionable inspiration. Be what you were meant to be and can be."

—Rishad Tobaccowala,
Author of *Restoring the Soul of Business* and *Re-Thinking Work*

"In *What Lights You Up?*, Mary Olson-Menzel masterfully transforms the concept of career building into an inspiring journey of self-discovery. With a pragmatic and empathetic voice, Mary's approach offers not just inspiration, but actionable steps to ensure that what lights you up guides you forward. Her blend of practical advice and personal reflection provides a structured roadmap to create a career you love. This book is a must-read for any professional looking to achieve fulfillment and find lasting passion in their work."

—Marshall Goldsmith,
Thinkers50 #1 Executive Coach and *New York Times* bestselling author of
The Earned Life, Triggers, and *What Got You Here Won't Get You There*

"Mary's generous spirit and infectious light shine through in this book. Whether you're looking to make a change or understand where you are, Mary's tips will guide you to better knowing yourself and owning your future."

—**Erica Hill,**
CNN Anchor and National Correspondent

"Mary Olson-Menzel has devoted her life to helping her clients find jobs and careers that align with their passion and provide the purpose that so many of us seek from our work. With this book she is now sharing her well-established methods with a broader audience. Anyone looking to be more fulfilled and engaged at work should do themselves a favor and read this book immediately."

—**Chris Farrell,**
Former Chief Strategy Officer of Mattel, Inc.

"This book is about so much more than just finding a good job or even the right fit. It's about finding meaningful and purposeful work that 'lights you up'—that you were meant for. And that's no easy task. But reading this book will set you on the right path."

—**Joshua Macht,**
President of the MassLive Media Group and
former CEO of Harvard Business Publishing

"Whether you're between jobs, just starting out, unhappy in your current role, or a seasoned professional, *What Lights You Up?* gives you critical tools to vastly improve your career path. Part workbook, part story, part reference guide, and part loving encouragement, this book will rekindle your hope and give you a winning edge to rise above the pack. With her unique mix of sunny optimism and practical advice, world-class business coach Mary Olson-Menzel walks you along her time-tested and proven path, showing you how to discover and land a job you love, or turn your current role into one that lights you up. This is the kind of book you'll want to keep handy and reference at every phase of your career. As Mary says, 'Don't give up before the magic sets in.' And to ignite that magic, all you need to do is pick up this book."

—**Victoria Labalme,**
Hall of Fame Speaker and *Wall Street Journal*
bestselling author of *Risk Forward*

WHAT LIGHTS YOU UP?

MARY OLSON-MENZEL

WHAT LIGHTS YOU UP?

Illuminate Your Path and Take the Next Big Step in Your Career

WILEY

Published by John Wiley & Sons, Inc., Hoboken, New Jersey.
Published simultaneously in Canada.

For general information on our other products and services or for technical support, please contact our Customer Care Department within the United States at (800) 762-2974, outside the United States at (317) 572-3993 or fax (317) 572-4002.

Wiley also publishes its books in a variety of electronic formats. Some content that appears in print may not be available in electronic formats. For more information about Wiley products, visit our web site at www.wiley.com.

Library of Congress Cataloging-in-Publication Data

Names: Olson-Menzel, Mary, author.
Title: What lights you up? : illuminate your path and take the next big
  step in your career / Mary Olson-Menzel.
Description: Hoboken, New Jersey : Wiley, [2024] | Includes index.
Identifiers: LCCN 2024025054 (print) | LCCN 2024025055 (ebook) | ISBN
  9781394267026 (hardback) | ISBN 9781394267040 (adobe pdf) | ISBN
  9781394267033 (epub)
Subjects: LCSH: Job hunting. | Vocational guidance.
Classification: LCC HF5382.7 .O47 2024 (print) | LCC HF5382.7 (ebook) |
  DDC 650.14—dc23/eng/20240701
LC record available at https://lccn.loc.gov/2024025054
LC ebook record available at https://lccn.loc.gov/2024025055

COVER DESIGN: PAUL MCCARTHY
COVER BACKGROUND: © GETTY IMAGES | PAKIN SONGMOR

SKY10082218_082124

This book is dedicated to my parents, Robert and Veronica, for teaching me how to love and encouraging me to follow my own light. To my son, Christopher, for reflecting that gift of light back to me, every single day. And to my husband, Dan, for holding down the fort through all of our adventures together. Also, to every client who has shared their journey with me. I am forever grateful.

Contents

Introduction		*xi*
Chapter 1	Identify Your Light	1
Chapter 2	Turn Your Light On	11
Chapter 3	Write Your Story	19
Chapter 4	Build Your Toolbox	31
Chapter 5	Follow Your Dream	39
Chapter 6	Tap into Your Network	45
Chapter 7	Choose Joy	55
Chapter 8	Develop Your Three Ps	61
Chapter 9	Shine in the Interview and Land the Job	83
Chapter 10	Succeed Today	101
Chapter 11	Create Forward Momentum	107
Chapter 12	Design a Framework for Success	113

Chapter 13   Give Yourself Grace   119

Chapter 14   Practice Gratitude   127

Conclusion: Lights on for Life   133

Exercises   139

Acknowledgments   183

About the Author   187

Notes   189

Index   191

Introduction

WHAT IF YOU could change your life for the better, simply by tapping into your own natural resources and being intentional about the direction you want to go now? I believe you can! Congratulations, you have just taken the first step towards a brighter future! Through the pages of this book, you will start looking at your life with fresh eyes. By tapping into your own "light source," you can design and follow the path to your next job and a more fulfilling career.

You bought this book for a reason, and I hope it inspires you to act and create a career path that lights you up. Let this book be your guide to your best career. And, most importantly, I want you to allow it to ignite your mind, illuminate your spirit, and keep the lights on in your heart.

I'm an executive coach—helping people thrive is my business. When people walk into my office, they often say they need help finding a job or getting promoted or that they just want more from their career and want to feel fulfilled and happy. I am lucky enough to have coached and guided hundreds of executives into more fulfilling careers and so many others down a path of creating a life and doing work that they love.

What you'll get in the pages of this book is, in part, what my coaching clients pay me top dollar for, and it lights me up to share it with you. I can't wait for you to dive in!

First and most fundamental, discovering what lights *you* up is vital. You must learn how to identify and to recognize what this is before sharing it with a potential employer. Because if you can't see it yourself, most likely neither can they. This is where your adventure begins.

Guiding people to see their own value and greatness is my passion and my dream for you. I know that when your light is on, you will:

- Get hired faster
- Get promoted faster
- Make more money
- Have a career that has meaning and brings you joy

If you were to hire me as your coach, the MVP 360 Pivot Program is what we would embark on together. This book is based on my proven methodology, but it's important to keep in mind that when working one on one with someone, a lot of the process gets customized to meet the needs of the specific client. It's an organic unfolding that leads us to places together that we might not have been able to imagine ourselves had we not worked together. I hope that the work you do throughout the pages of this book takes you on a journey to places you have always dreamed about and beyond!

MVP 360 Pivot Program

Go deep: Who are you? The first step is taking the time to get to know yourself. We look at your life from a holistic perspective: financial, professional, and personal. We begin to help align your dreams with reality.

Personal brand: What is it that makes you unique? Why should an organization hire you over someone else with the exact same experience? What are your strengths and how can you "sell" them? What is your elevator pitch?

Positioning: What is your personal brand in the market? In addition to a strong resume, a robust, professional online profile is key.

Explore: Where do you see yourself? We work with you to design a target list that we call the Three Ps of places you want to work. We encourage you to think strategically and to look at all potential options and ideas with a fresh lens.

Expand: How can you tap your network? We help you think expansively about how to utilize the power of networking on all fronts. We encourage you to think outside of the box and go for it.

Opening doors: How do you find the best fit for you? We help navigate through the confusion and noise and find the right approach to every unique opportunity.

Preparation and rehearsals: How can you stand out from the rest? We work diligently to help you prepare for interviews and for every networking opportunity created. We want you to be prepared and put your best foot forward to "wow" the hiring managers.

Connection and support for success: How can we best support you? We are with our clients every step of the way to help you navigate and foster relationships that will lead to your next opportunity. Throughout the entire process, we are by your side, as a resource and a coach. We are also here to help you navigate and negotiate an offer that is a win-win for you and the organization. We stay close to you even after you have accepted the new position. We stay connected and offer ongoing coaching to help you adjust and excel in your new role, creating lasting success for your future.

You will see this process as you move through the pages and the exercises of this book. The world continues to evolve and the way people work is changing rapidly, and this in turn creates tremendous opportunity. Many of us get to choose how and where we work. Gone are the days of working 9 to 5 and celebrating 25 years at one company with a gold watch. Our work lives look different now, and more often employees are calling the shots about what that looks like. What's different now is that people have proven that they can be trusted to be even more productive, creative, and efficient when their needs are honored in a way that resonates with them.

People are standing up and saying, "I am valuable to this organization and I want to work on my own terms." Companies have been forced into a new frontier where the employee experience matters more than ever.

You deserve to love what you do! Your life is too precious to work in a place or a profession doing something that doesn't give you joy. Just remember, no job is perfect, but if you follow the 80/20 rule—80% good stuff and 20% stuff you don't necessarily love to do—you will be off to a good (and realistic!) start.

When I was a little girl, my parents told me that I could do whatever I wanted to do in life. I still wonder whether they believed that for themselves. Their story is a big part of why I do what I do today, and why it is imperative that you keep your lights on in your work and your heart—for your sake, and for the sake of all those who love you.

When I started this book, quite a few years ago, it was a different world than what it is today, but one thing remains the same: doing what lights you up is of the utmost importance in your career. The world of work will keep changing but that timeless truth is evergreen. At times we are pivoting, sometimes growing, sometimes flowing, and now we are transforming. Welcome to your transformation.

Throughout this book, I will be sharing wisdom and knowledge through quotes and excerpts from others who have an undeniable light in their work, so I'd like to start you out with this one.

"The whole secret of a successful life is to find out what is one's destiny to do, and then do it."

—*Henry Ford*

Enjoy the ride!

WHAT LIGHTS YOU UP?

1

Identify Your Light

"Every great dream begins with a dreamer. Always remember, you have within you the strength, the patience, and the passion to reach for the stars to change the world."

—Harriet Tubman

THANK YOU FOR picking up this book! It is true that everyone needs a little help now and then—and even the most successful people understand that a coach makes them even better. My very first "coaches" were my parents, guiding the way through my childhood. As I was growing up, my parents were a fascinating balance of creativity and business savvy. This created a stable and happy childhood for me. When my parents were happy, I felt safe and loved.

My mother was 42 when she had me; she tells me that having my little sister and me later in her life has kept her young, but I disagree. Maybe that was part of it, but there is so much more. She was an artist, a dancer, and a force to be reckoned with. When I was growing up, she taught art to our local community and attended art fairs around the region, selling her original pieces to art collectors far and wide. She was happy. As I write this book, I know now that doing what she loved is what kept her young for so many years.

When she passed away at the age of 98 in March of 2024, as I was finishing this book, her body was not as strong as it once was, but when she smiled, she still had a beautiful sparkle in her eyes and her soul, especially when she was doing what she loved or with the people she loved. Her hands were shaky near the end and it was harder for her to do the fine art that she used to do, so later in her life she pivoted to doing collage and abstract watercolor. It's gorgeous and it made her light up as she continued to create beautiful art right up until the days before she passed. I was continually amazed by her creativity, her spirit, and her grit and the way she would throw her hands up in the air to greet me with such love and enthusiasm, every time I walked in the door.

I remember Mom as beautiful; she always was. When I was a child, she would walk into a room and people would notice. She had short, dark, and very stylish hair. Her eyes sparkled even when she wasn't smiling. She was filled with life, and she knew it, and so did everyone who met her. Even until her last day, she wore a flower in her hair and a twinkle in her eyes and people still noticed when she walked into a room at the retirement community where she lived. When I visited her in the days right before she died, she could still manage to throw her hands up in the air to greet me and do her dancing to the best of her abilities from her chair!

When I was in first grade, she came into my classroom to teach my classmates and me how to hula dance, the Hukilau, grass skirt, and all! I still remember it so vividly. My childhood friends constantly remind me how much fun she was when we were all growing up. At a recent Barrington High School reunion, a 50-something-year-old man (and my first-grade classmate) told me that learning the hula with my mom was one of the highlights of his entire first-grade experience. Even then, my mom's light was shining brightly for all my classmates to see. This authentic and true inner light was noticed by all, both young and old. This created a memory that made a lot of people remember my mom many years later.

Your inner light is your secret sauce. It's what makes you memorable and draws people to you. While the hope is that it will be seen and remembered by potential employers, the fortunate coincidence is that it will also be noticed by people in all areas of your life. Everyone around you will benefit from your inner light once you truly let it shine. Think about this. What is it that makes you memorable? How can you tap into that energy?

The world of work has forever changed and will continue to change. The good news is that what employers are looking for has changed, too, for the better. It's no longer just about your skill set and what you know how to do. It's also about who you are and what you bring to the team. You have an asset that you may have not even considered. It's not your hard skills or technical knowledge per se, but your soft skills and human qualities. It's what I call your *light* that gets those skills recognized front and center. And it's your light that gets you hired.

We are moving into a new future of work and it's exciting because it's your work and your future!

What if where you are today, right this very minute, is the perfect place to start a new dream and create a new plan for your career? I say it is. And I will keep reminding you in the pages of this book that you can do this, no matter your starting point.

Start today and you can begin to act right now, with no more time spent on regrets or the mistakes of your past. Mistakes are just an opportunity for reflection and growth if we choose to see them that way.

As you read through the chapters of this book, you can begin again and again, creating a new path for your career and your life.

In the world of work, to stay relevant and successful, organizations and people have to reinvent themselves regularly, and that has never been truer than it is now. There is a sea change in the way that we work and do business. With this change, the geographic playing field has expanded and what were once limiting boundaries have gone away. There is more opportunity across the globe for us all if we choose to open our hearts and minds to see it. Technology has opened the doors—whether we are in the office or on our couches, we can talk and work with people all over the world.

This book is about lighting up your career and recognizing the possibilities right in front of you or maybe even just around the corner. It's about opening up your heart and digging deeply into your passions and what you are uniquely gifted to do, just because it's who you are.

Two hundred people can apply for the same VP of sales job. They can have excellent credentials, maybe even many from the same schools and companies, but what is it that makes that one person stand out and get hired? It is in identifying what it is that lights you up and then letting that unique light shine by being true to yourself in the interview. That is why you are here today, reading the pages in this book: to allow your inner light to shine in the workplace and to bring authenticity to work every day.

There is so much more to all of us than what we see on the outside or on a CV, and this book is for you—you as the whole person, all parts of you.

You get to play with your own shades of greatness here. As an example, I am a daughter, a sister, a wife, a mom, and a friend, but I am also a seasoned executive, an entrepreneur, a business owner, and an executive coach.

My father was a businessman and entrepreneur, with a big creative brain and a big heart. My earliest memories of my father, though, did not revolve around business. They were memories of being outdoors, boating, learning to fish, and camping in northern Wisconsin. He was much more subdued than my mom, quieter, with a quick wit and dry sense of humor. When my dad said something, it was usually substantial. He was constantly giving my siblings and me experiential history lessons by road-tripping with all of us in our wood-paneled Chrysler station wagon to all the state capitals. As a result, we not only knew all the capitals of the United States, but by the time we got to high school, we had visited most of them!

Dad wouldn't ever be caught wearing a hula skirt or teaching my class the Hukilau, but he used his unique light, intellect, and creativity to teach me about life. He instilled a value system in me, a moral compass to help light my way as I matured.

The first time I had a sense of what my dad did for work I was probably around ten years old. He was on the phone with an advertiser or client, and I remember him talking about Dr. Pepper, reciting the company's old slogan, "I'm a Pepper, you're a Pepper, wouldn't you like to be a Pepper, too?" I was drawn in, fascinated. The next call I heard was him talking about being in "good hands" with Allstate. Did he make that up?! Did he write the slogans for what I was seeing on TV? Wow, some of them he did, not the Dr Pepper ad, but apparently my dad was on the team that created the slogan "You're in good hands with Allstate." To this day, that slogan is still used over and over, through the decades since they created it. And every time I see an Allstate ad on TV, I smile and think of him.

Life with my parents and many siblings was always interesting. Our house was full of life, with lots of energy and personalities!

And then something happened that changed our lives forever. My father took over his father's company, which meant stepping out of a career that he loved in advertising to take on the responsibility of the family business. We still had a lovely life but, as I got older, I started to realize that my father had given up his dreams and passions. He stepped out of his light to bear the burden of responsibility, running the family business for his father, taking care of his children (all six of us!), and even his siblings.

This new job was a change for my dad, and he went from creative executive (think *Mad Men*) to business operations. He had to walk away from his dream and learn how to run the business. It was a tough transition and it showed in his eyes, in his demeanor, and his attitude.

Then Dad asked Mom to stop doing what she loved to help him with the family business. I can only imagine that this might have been one of the hardest things he had ever done, asking my mom for help, especially as a man who prided himself on being the provider for our family. At that moment, I imagined my mom felt terrible, having to give up time with us as well as doing what she loved.

I now realize that it was at that point in my childhood that I witnessed both of my parents' lights go out. Their dreams were interrupted by the weight of responsibility in carrying the family business. Working at the family business was not a good match for either of them at a soul level, but they both did it, out of deep responsibility to my father's family and us. I didn't know it at the time, but this was likely the beginning of the end of their marriage. They divorced many years later, and I sometimes think it was because they were both forced to give up doing what they loved.

Watching the lights in my parent's eyes go out to keep the lights on in our home was hard to process intellectually at such a young age. I felt it deep in my heart and it was palpable in our home. This book will give you the tools to make sure that your light doesn't dim the way my parents' did.

This is a very real situation for so many, needing to provide for yourself and possibly your entire family. So how do you do so? What if a job cannot provide that for you and you feel trapped? Keep moving toward what it is that lights you up. You can also achieve this by starting a "side hustle" (with something you are passionate about—we will go much deeper into this in Chapter 13).

My experience as a child, is a big part of who I am today and the reason that I chose the path that I did. The early years, watching everything in my childhood home, shaped me so very much. Even at a fairly young age I knew that I wanted to chart my own course. I never wanted to lose my passion or my spirit like my parents did. And I know they didn't want me to, either.

This is what drives me, following my path and creating a life that I love.

I don't want you to shortchange your light for a job; it is your life, and your life is important. You matter.

You might be at a turning point or a fork in the road and wondering which way to go. You might be in your first job, or your fourth job, or even your tenth job. It doesn't matter where you are. You want more; you know in your heart you've got more to give and more to do. Please recognize that doing what you love and what lights you up inside is your best chance of having a truly fulfilling career and life.

It is your *real business*, and your *real responsibility*, to follow a path that includes doing what you love using your unique skills and attending to the wants, needs, desires, and circumstances you are in right now. This book will help you discover what that unique path looks like for you.

In more than 30 years of working with people, I have seen the vast difference between those who are filled with light and those who have let their lights dim.

- People with their "lights on" get hired.
- People with their "lights on" get promoted.
- People with their "lights on" are statistically happier and healthier.

You're embarking on a powerful journey throughout the pages of this book. You will start to see a path unfold ahead of you—read on, do the work, and be honest with yourself. Answer the questions to the best of your ability in the order that you read them. Go at a pace that feels right for you.

This is not timed or graded. This is your life and only you will know the cadence of how fast or how slowly you go.

Take your time, take a break when you need to, and just keep going.

At times it will feel inspiring and exciting, and there may also be a question or two that make you feel a bit uncomfortable. Sit with that and get accustomed to exploring the deepest parts of you, the shadows and the light. It's all good. Without the shadows, you would not cherish the light as much. Whatever feelings you have as you read on and do the work, know that you are on the path of discovery, the path of reigniting your work—and your life.

What the World Needs Now Is Your Special Light

How do you stand out in the crowd? By tapping into doing what you love and bringing your true self to work. That's your invisible superpower where no other person can compete. It is what lights you up that creates passion, and it is how you can create more excitement and purpose in your work—for yourself, your company, and your future.

Being true to who you are in your work is imperative. You may even take your most significant assets for granted because "it's just who you are," but others might see it as what sets you apart.

You know that feeling when someone walks into a room, and people sit up straighter and take notice? There's just something about them that you can't quite put your finger on, but you know that you'd like some of it for yourself. Many call it charisma or the "it factor." That special something is what I call light, and it is unique to you alone. You will feel it when you're standing in your truth and owning who you are.

You are the only one with this specific blueprint of light, and there are no imitations; nothing and no one else is created quite like you. And the world needs you to be brave enough to elevate your gifts, bring them to life, and bring them to others.

Unless we are independently wealthy, most of us have to work. It's essential to be able to pay our bills and keep the lights on in our home. Remember, it's not all about the money, but having enough money to survive and hopefully thrive is important. We all want to be able to pay our bills and put food on the table for our family. But after our basic human needs are met, money becomes subjective. Pay is not only about financial dividends; it can also come from deep contentment that comes at the end of the day. You can bring more joy into your workday because it's more fun to do work that you love. It's gratifying to know that what you do is making an impact in some small way. If it lights you up, then it is worth more than dollars alone.

Your *passion*, your *purpose*, your *skills*, and your *personality* will equal your *paycheck*.

When you start to realize what makes you tick and begin to do what you love, your work will never be the same, and neither will you. When you understand what lights you up and are doing it regularly, you'll want more and more of that feeling. And you will continue to attract more good stuff and exciting things will start to happen for you; that's the law of the Universe.

As an added bonus, your light will illuminate the others around you. And that joy and satisfaction you feel will remind you to keep the lights on in your heart so they can transfer right into your work and spill over into your whole life. It's the direct correlation with creating a more fulfilling future for yourself. You will start to recognize the difference between a mediocre or "just okay" career and one that makes your heart sing.

Companies are made up of people, and it's the people who set them apart. Without the right people in place, even the best product can fail. People are the key, always. Never forget that.

Many employers want people who will be innovative, thrive in uncertainty, and bring new solutions to the table. Companies and hiring managers depend on people who come to work with their lights on, and this includes:

- Emotional intelligence
- Mental agility
- Poise and presence
- Humor
- Kindness
- Creativity
- Empathy

And so much more, whatever you have that brings a unique perspective to bring real solutions to the table. These are the characteristics that will help drive organizations into a successful future.

Summary

Your inner light is your secret sauce. Everyone around you will benefit from your inner light once you truly let it shine. The world of work has forever changed. Your soft skills are as important as your practical skill set, and your inner light illuminates these things and more. Don't hesitate any longer to find it.

Seeing my parents' lights go out midway through their careers to be responsible successors to my grandfather was jarring. I can only imagine the things both my mother and father could have done if they didn't have to bear the burden of the family business. This turning point in my early life forever informed the way I look at work and success. I don't want you to shortchange your light for a job like so many have and do. It's your life, and it's important. This is your *real business*, and your *real responsibility*, to follow a path that includes doing what you love using your unique skills and attending to the wants, needs, desires, and circumstances you are in right now.

What the world needs now is your special light. Your *passion*, your *purpose*, your *skills*, and your *personality* will equal your *paycheck*.

2

Turn Your Light On

"To shine your brightest light is to be who you truly are."

—Roy T. Bennett

YOU ARE HERE to shine your light. That is your number-one job. Your light is a gift that you've had since the day you were born. When you see young children, you see that most are naturally vibrant and filled with light since they have fewer filters in their relatively short lives. As a result, they are more connected to their true essence.

Figuring out what lights you up will help you see past the filters and/or self-limiting beliefs that you've accumulated over time and will help you reconnect to your true essence. Our great challenge as we grow older is to stay connected to that light in our hearts and to bring that luminous energy into our work.

Your unique light is *exactly* what employers are looking for. Your light is what will set you apart from the rest of the crowd. Every. Single. Time.

Employers have told me repeatedly that they would hire someone with fewer skills if they had the right mindset and energy. Savvy hiring managers know that skills can be taught but that this light energy comes from within. Your light is perceived as a positive energy that radiates from within you and impacts all that you do and everyone and everything around you. When you bring your light to work with you, magic happens in your career.

11

At the Tribune Company, I was hired as the head of recruitment and I worked with all of the executive leaders across the country as their business partner for recruiting and hiring new executives and then onboarding them for success. At one point I oversaw a nation-wide search for a new head of sales for our flagship property. We interviewed many qualified and talented executives, and then there was Ken. He came from the scrappy "number-two" ranked paper in town, located just down the street from our majestic Tribune Tower. Ken did not have an MBA from a top school like the other candidates we were interviewing, but he was "lit up"—from the inside out. He was the one who stood out above the rest, not necessarily because of his resume, but because of his energy. Ken had charisma. He could breathe life into any room and he radiated an authenticity and an undeniable positive energy.

The hiring manager had a big decision to make: hire the most "qualified" candidate because of their resume and pedigree, or hire the other guy, from down the street, who brought an enormous, bright, shining energy into the room. My boss ended up hiring Ken, making what I believe might have been the wisest hiring decision of his career. By choosing a candidate with a magnetic personality, a strong inner light, and an honest work ethic, he breathed new life into the entire sales department.

As our flagship property's new head of sales, Ken invigorated the entire department and increased revenue exponentially. Subsequently, he got promoted many times within our organization, eventually ending up as president of several of our national media properties. He became a dear friend, and even 20 years later he can still light up a room just by being himself.

As Ken's example illustrates, your light is how you get noticed. Your light is what sets you apart from someone who might just have come from a better school or has deeper work experience.

As you might imagine, Ken is still enjoying his work and doing quite well. He recently told me, "Hard work puts you where good luck can find you. Mary, like you, I want to do everything I do with passion and I want to make a difference every day. I want to be as kind as possible and help make people's days better. That's how I go through life. Every single day."

Getting Started

Before we dive in, I recommend that you get a notebook you can dedicate solely to completing the exercises in this book and to documenting this new journey you're on as it unfolds. There are also worksheets at the back of the book you can use to help you. Take this book with you everywhere you go if you want, and keep it handy so you can refer back to your thoughts on a regular basis. You'll be using it and reflecting on your work throughout the process.

While you might be tempted to just use your phone or computer to take notes, I do not recommend this. It has been scientifically proven that your brain is better able to process thoughts and ideas when you put pen to paper. There is data that shows that writing by hand offers significant benefits over typing, especially when it comes to learning, remembering, and being creative. In a 2024 *Inc.* magazine article,[1] Professor Audrey van der Meer, a brain researcher at the Norwegian University of Science and Technology and co-author of the study, says, "We show that when writing by hand, brain connectivity patterns are far more elaborate than when typewriting on a keyboard. Such widespread brain connectivity is known to be crucial for memory formation and for encoding new information and, therefore, is beneficial for learning." According to *Inc.*, writing instead of typing will help you slow down and think more, thus enabling you to use more of your brain and senses in the process.

As you answer the questions throughout this book and record your thoughts, or even draw a few pictures or doodles, I hope you have fun, too, as new possibilities and ideas come to light. As you work through this book, you'll be able to refer to and reflect on these notes to discover even more about yourself and your goals as you move forward in this journey. At times, the process of reflection and self-discovery can sometimes be a little daunting, but it can also be a creative and fun activity.

Trust the first answers that come to you. Let your intuition be your guide and let the pen flow on the paper. No editing or interpretation is necessary at this point, although it may be tempting. This is not a time to be perfect and there are no wrong answers. I suggest you approach this part of the process more like a brainstorming session, a free-flowing time of self-expression.

Take the time to recognize on a deeper level who you truly are, moving forward at a pace that is comfortable for you. Don't forget to give yourself credit for every step you take!

To find what lights you up, you'll have to dig deep to uncover what makes you tick and what brings you joy. The following exercises are designed to jumpstart your journey of self-discovery and to help you to think about yourself differently. You can do this—it's an investment in your self and your future!

Exercise 1   Finding Your Light

Jot down the answers to the following questions.

What Is Your Current Employment Situation?
- Are you employed today? (Yes or no)
- Do you have a vision of what your next job looks like?
- How much money do you need to make to keep the lights on in your home?
- How much do you realistically want to earn this year?
- What kind of a work/life balance do you need?

What Makes You Unique?
- List three words that best describe what makes you unique. Think of qualities that you like about yourself. This could be in the context of work or at home.
- Describe your sense of generosity, curiosity, and flexibility.
- Describe your sense of humor.
- Describe yourself as a problem-solver, or someone who can get things done with efficiency.
- Describe your abilities around kindness, empathy, and care about people.
- Describe how you embrace a positive attitude in work.
- Describe how you use your intuitive abilities at work.

- Describe how your listening skills enhance your performance.
- Describe what qualities might set you apart from others at work or at home?
- List three things that you are most proud of, in your personal and/or professional life. This can include accomplishments, activities, skills, behaviors, and so on.

If you have a hard time identifying this, ask a friend or a family member. These qualities typically come so easily to you that you might not even think of them, but they do lead you to your light.

What Are Your Interests and Hobbies?

- List things that interest you and keep your light on. This could include anything from mentoring junior employees at your organization to running a 5K for charity. Do you have a side hustle, a passion you're doing in the hours when you're not working, such as photography, art, or music, or perhaps traveling, speaking another language, hiking, boating, or yoga, for example?

What's on Your Bucket List?

- Put together a list of things you've done in the past that you now look back on with joy and gratitude, and then prepare a bucket list of what you would like to do in the future. For example, when I was younger, I was passionate about scuba diving and have had the amazing opportunity to dive in five different countries and many beautiful locations around the world. As I've gotten older, I've become a little more risk-averse and so the scuba has shifted to snorkeling and hiking. One of my current bucket list items is to travel with my family to all seven continents. *Another bucket list item of mine was to write this book.*

There are no rules when it comes to your list. No matter how big or how small, if it's something you've done that gave you joy, or something you'd like to do, then put it on this list. Have fun with this, let yourself dream, and enjoy the process as it unfolds!

What Are Your Passions and Dreams?

- What did you dream of doing as a child?
- Was there any specific job you wanted to do when you grew up?
- What aspects of your past or current jobs are related to your childhood dreams?
- Is your job at all related to what you thought you wanted to do when you were younger?
- What are your dreams now, and have they changed since you were a child?
- What are you most passionate about right now?
- What makes you the happiest right now?

Identifying what makes you happy or what you are passionate about are *huge* questions, and sometimes difficult to answer. As adults, many of us have forgotten how to answer these questions because we're so busy checking off tasks from our to-do lists during our daily lives that we rarely take the time to think about ourselves or what makes us truly happy anymore.

Do not get frustrated if you don't have an answer right away. Take whatever time you need to think about how to answer these questions truthfully. Let these thoughts marinate, percolate, and simmer deep in your heart. I remember a time when it was hard for me to answer these questions, too. We are all at different stages of our unfolding, so go easy on yourself.

If you are truly stuck, as I mentioned before, I will always recommend consulting with family and friends to get their opinions, too. Putting together your own "advisory board" of trusted family and friends who have your best interests at heart is a great idea, no matter what stage of life you're in. They will help shine the mirror back at you and help keep you honest. Identifying your natural gifts and deepest desires in truthful and thoughtful answers will lead you toward your best path!

Exercise 2   What Brings You Joy? Create Your Light Log

A lot of my clients struggle with this one. Some are so caught up in the responsibility, the "have-tos" and the "should-dos," that the idea of figuring out what brings them joy can sometimes be difficult.

Throw away the old mindset that work is just work and can't be fun. The truth is, when you're doing what you love, work can be so much fun!

My business partner Mel Shahbazian and I sometimes pinch ourselves because we have so much fun at work, especially when we're working together. I'm not saying we don't work hard, because we do, but it's so much better when you not only love what you do but can also find joy in the moments of your day-to-day work life.

Hint: Finding the right people to work with really helps a lot. So look carefully at the culture and the people of every organization that you talk with and ask yourself, "Would I enjoy working with these people?" When you're working with great people and in a culture that will support its people to grow and thrive, it not only makes work more fun, but challenges you to bring your best self to work, too. As you move forward, look for people and companies that are like-minded in values, visions, and goals.

We are here to find solutions for a better job, career, and life. Once you get over any limiting thought patterns or ideas about yourself or what work "should be" you can relax into the process and start to let it unfold. If this is something you struggle with, just know that you are not alone.

Create a Daily Light Log

Make a list of all the things that bring you joy. It doesn't have to be just the big things; you can start small, with the simple pleasures in life. It can be as easy as enjoying a good cup of coffee, or your dog greeting you with kisses after your morning run. It might even be a partner, child, or friend giving you a much-needed hug. Even the pleasure of crossing items off your to-do list can bring joy and satisfaction to your day. Whatever it is, list it, and keep paying attention throughout your day to anything that brings a smile to your face!

As you start to list things in your daily Light Log, you'll start to see recurring themes, which will make it easier to identify what lights you up. This is such an important exercise and one that not only helps us to identify what lights us up but also reminds us to be grateful for all the things both big and small that bring us joy and make us smile. When we are grateful for even the smallest of moments, more things to be grateful for and opportunities to be grateful about tend to show up in our lives.

Hint: Creating a Light Log will also help you in later chapters when I ask you to create a target list of companies for your career search.

Understanding what you want out of a career and learning how to articulate your strengths and goals to a future employer is an important part of the journey. On the flipside, as I mentioned, this is also quite helpful in identifying the right kind of cultural fit in any organization you are interviewing with.

Now take a nice deep breath and congratulate yourself on not only learning more about yourself but also taking important first steps in your journey to find a job where you can let your light shine brightly!

For more exercises and exclusive teachings, visit: MaryOlsonMenzel.com/Resources

Summary

Our great challenge as we grow older is to stay connected to the light in our hearts and to bring that luminous energy into our work. Your unique light is exactly what employers are looking for. Your light is what will set you apart from the rest of the crowd.

If you begin to doubt your qualifications for a role that lights you up, remember my friend Ken. His charisma and energy made him stand out compared to the slate of candidates whose backgrounds closely fit the job description. Ken earned the job not only with his skills but with his passion and strong inner light. And then Ken took those attributes and breathed life into his new role and his department.

Prepare yourself to find and explore your inner light with a physical notebook and pen, leveraging more of your senses than by simply using a computer. When you're ready, Exercises 1 and 2, "Finding Your Light" and "Create Your Light Log," will be a good start to your journey. Remember throughout this process to trust the first answers that come to you. There are no wrong answers. This is a free-flowing time of self-expression and step one to get you closer to identifying "what lights you up."

3

Write Your Story

"The privilege of a lifetime is being who you are."

—Joseph Campbell

A Resume Tells; a Story Sells

Your resume tells the facts. How you describe your career journey and job history is the story that will get an interviewer excited about you. In addition to your resume, I believe that a good story is one of the most critical tools in landing your next job. A good resume outlines your qualifications to get you in the door, but it does not adequately help a potential employer to see your unique style and personality.

In Chapter 4 we'll examine the nuts and bolts of your resume and a few tips for your job search toolbox, but for now let's have some fun telling the story of who you are and why you do what you do!

In the previous chapters, you spent some time dreaming; now we start to create. Let's craft the authentic and fascinating story of who you are and how you got to where you are today. If you tell me that your story is not fascinating, I will tell you that every person and every story is interesting and worth telling. So don't get intimidated by what might seem like a boring story to you, because it's yours, and to someone else, it could be fascinating.

Stories help others to understand the qualities that make you stand out from the rest, which might just put you over the finish line as the best candidate for the job. As a result, I always recommend to my clients that they work to develop a compelling story or personal narrative to share with a potential employer in an interview. Stories illustrate not only who you were, but who you are, and who you strive to be. Your story is the progression and evolution of who you are and why someone would want to hire you.

Storytelling is a much more effective strategy to make a personal connection with a potential employer than a resume alone. People connect with stories. A well-crafted and authentic story can be very powerful. The information and facts presented in your resume help employers check the boxes, but it is the stories that make us human and we are all human beings working together to make any organization better. Stories have been with us since the dawn of time. Our brains are wired to tell stories and make connections. From the primitive versions of storytelling around campfires, spurring the earliest conversations known to humans, to an informal interview in a coffeehouse today, the formula is the same.

Employers want to know about your journey, what makes you tick, what lights you up, and why you would be interested in working for them. Stories help to illustrate these things. They connect us on a more personal level, which eventually leads employers to want to hire you.

If at this point you're doubting yourself because you don't believe you're a good storyteller, read on. I have exercises coming up to help you develop your narrative. Please remember that you do have a story—a compelling one, one that could lead you to your next great job! Sometimes it's hard to recognize that until you put pen to paper.

Every Experience Has Led You to Where You Are Today

Focus on creating a story based on your unique professional journey. You will develop a narrative you can share during the interview process that will resonate with potential employers.

Let's start by looking at the many decisions you have made in your life, both personal and professional, and what you have accomplished thus far. Do not get discouraged if you feel like you haven't accomplished a lot. Every single experience, whether positive or negative, has impacted you in ways both large and small, resulting in the person you are today. I believe that what people remember the most about you is not what's on your resume, but rather the story of who you are and what makes you special.

Who you are as a human being is your differentiator, not whether you can build an Excel spreadsheet or create a strategic plan!

Start at the Beginning

The best way to approach your story is to just start from the beginning (birth, childhood, high school, college). Choose whatever seems like the most relevant starting point to create a picture of who you are and what brings you to where you are today, and work chronologically. This is always the easiest way to begin.

When you describe where you started and then explain how you got to where you are today, it's much easier for people to follow your trajectory. It's your story. So if something important comes to mind that you did as a child, teenager, or young adult, start there. I prefer to see where you got your start and learn about the choices you made along the way. It's interesting and relevant to understand why you made the moves that you did at each juncture in your life.

For example, if your first job was mowing lawns and you are now a landscape architect, that might be relevant to include in your story. Likewise, if your first job was babysitting or you were the oldest child who regularly cared for your siblings and you are now a teacher, that might be relevant to include.

- College and trade school decisions are also important to include.
- What dreams or ambitions led you to choose a particular college, trade school, and/or major?
- Did you change your major, and if so, why? (Many people do!)

You are allowed to change your mind at any juncture as long as you can explain why you did it. Several of my family members are a perfect example of changing majors that led to personal success.

My brother, John, loved nature and drawing from an early age. The cartoons and pictures he drew while we were growing up were spectacular. He left Chicago at the age of 18 to head to Utah State University with a major in wildlife science and a minor in art. He quickly realized that his happy place—where he felt the most "lit up"—was at the easel painting the wildlife and nature that he so dearly loved, so he switched his major to art. He is one of the most gifted artists I know, and he is so in the "flow" and at peace while painting that he literally loses track of time. He can light up a blank canvas like no one else. I'm in awe every time I see his work.

My sister, Tricia, followed in my mom's footsteps and started as a dance major, transferred to a different university her junior year, changed her major quite a few times (five times to be exact!), and ended up going to law school and working as a lawyer. It's a great story, and one that people remember when she tells it, with plenty of twists and turns to get her from dancer to successful immigration lawyer.

My stepdaughter, Sam, originally went to college to pursue an early childhood education major. As one of our community's most popular babysitters, she adored children and so we thought that she had found her calling. Midway through her sophomore year, she decided to change her major to social work and minor in family sciences. Even though she knew this career path would mean less money, she followed her heart and trusted her instincts. We fully supported her choice, and I am confident that she will be successful because she pivoted to a career path that lights her up.

My niece, Paige, did something similar. She started as a pre-med major, but after a few semesters she felt that it wasn't for her. Unsure of her new direction, she spent the summer interning at my company and had the opportunity to do several of the exercises in this book as well as some deep soul-searching. As a result, she decided to pursue her interest in marketing and media. From a young age she was always very creative, so this was no surprise to me. She changed her major to marketing/PR and recently completed her MBA, graduating summa cum laude with almost straight As. Following her light not only led her to academic success but to a choice of several job offers, and she is working in a career that she enjoys and where she has found great success.

Every Journey Has Twists and Turns

Most of us haven't had a straightforward career path. We all experience twists and turns or setbacks and even make bad career choices from time to time.

I want you to understand that there are no regrets here. The past is the past. If you believe one of these setbacks is relevant to include in your story, then you should emphasize what you learned from the experience, how it has shaped you into who you are today, and how it has better prepared you for your future. Anything that stands out, you should be prepared to discuss. For example, if there is an unexplained gap, you want to be prepared with answers about why.

The tool that doesn't change or "go out of style" is your story.

Sometimes, people struggle with self-promoting during an interview. In fact, studies have found that females are less inclined to promote themselves, even for a job, than males. "According to a recent National Bureau of Economic Research working paper, women consistently rated their performance on a test lower than did men, even though both groups had the same average score."[1]

No matter your gender, work experience, or confidence level, you must get comfortable with telling your story and speaking to your best qualities, highlighting your strengths, and doing it in a compelling and authentic way. You can practice in front of a mirror, a trusted friend, or a coach. I highly suggest doing all three!

The purpose of an interview is to sell yourself in a truthful and honest way. You don't want to portray someone that you are not, but you do want to get the job if you feel it is the right job for you. This is your chance to let your light shine and let that interviewer see your true essence. That will be the part that carries you across the finish line and into the job of your dreams.

You don't want to stretch the truth in the interview. Remember, you don't have to check all the boxes on the description to get the job; you just have to shine your own light into the process. When you can articulate who you are and what makes you special with honesty, you are also better able to discern whether this company is a good fit for you.

Employers want to know about your journey, what makes you tick, what lights you up, and why you would be interested in working for them. They want to be delightfully surprised, impressed, inspired, curious, and maybe even a bit disarmed. *You want to be remembered when you walk out of that interview,* for the unique light that you would bring to whatever role it is that you are looking for as your next job. Just like my first-grade classmates remembered when my mom did the hula. Well—maybe a little more professionally inspired—but you get the picture!

I know an executive, Jeremy Cage, who took a year off to sail around the world with his family. He ended up stepping away from a career he loved to take this adventure, and his company welcomed him back after his 18-month sabbatical. What an amazing journey he had, and he ended up writing a great book called *All Dreams on Deck* about following dreams, and he inspired a lot of people in the process, by following his own dreams.

Some of the most accomplished executives I know have taken a few sidesteps, some strategic and some due to outside circumstances, to get to their current success. Taking the path less traveled is not only okay, but also what makes you *you.*

I love to hear stories where there are interesting twists and turns along the way. In most people's reality, their career path looks something like the image seen here.

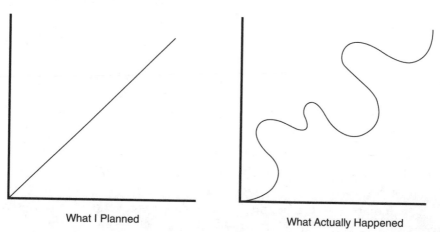

What I Planned   What Actually Happened

Whatever the twists and turns your journey has taken you on thus far, be grateful because it's what has brought you to where you are today. Most of us have taken quite a circuitous path to get to where we are today, and that is okay. Life happens to all of us, and many of us have had to pivot as circumstances change, such as with child rearing or caring for elderly parents. This is all a part of the journey, and part of the school of life.

One of my biggest "upsets" (or what I now call "pivots") happened when I was in my 20s and set me on the path that led me to where I am today. When I graduated from college, I became a television reporter. That was my dream. I was so happy. My innate curiosity about people and quest to find the "scoop" and create a well-written story made me perfect for this role. Running from story to story in the field with my cameraman, I would look for the best story and visuals and bring it back for Channel 6 to run on the nightly news. I loved it, but I was also settled in Chicago at the time with my fiancé, Kurt, and didn't want to constantly chase the next story or move to a new broadcast market for a job.

So I pivoted. I had a vision that if I did not report the news for a living, I wanted to work for Leo Burnett, just like my dad. Leo Burnett was one of the largest advertising agencies at the time and was based in Chicago. After eight interviews, I came so close, but did not get the job. I was the runner-up and they hired someone else. I was devastated.

I allowed myself to feel the feelings but then I brushed off my resume and stayed hopeful. I persevered and kept going to interviews to find my next job, and in one serendipitous interview, a senior recruiter named Rich B. saw something in me. He knew I could take my interviewing skills that I was using as a television reporter and my desire to help people and learn the skills necessary to be a recruiter. He believed in me, took me under his wing, and taught me to recruit in the hottest industry in the world at the time, the tech industry.

So I made the first pivot of my career very early on and ended up falling into recruiting. I realized that what lit me up was learning about what others loved and wanted and matching them to the perfect job. I found that learning about people and what drives them to do what they do, and then helping them find a job, was what lit me up. It was also more money than being a reporter and I got to stay in Chicago. Extra bonus!

No memorable story is ever all positive with hearts and rainbows. At some point or another, we all overcome hardships that result in developing new strength and resilience. People enjoy hearing this and are inspired by the stories of overcoming adversity—it creates an interesting narrative and speaks to your ability to learn from your experiences, your courage, and your honesty. Sharing our personal stories allows us to connect with potential employers on a personal level that wouldn't otherwise be possible through a resume.

Make It Personal

Weave in as many personal stories as appropriate, stories that will highlight your strengths and character, whenever possible. This helps to make your story not only more interesting but also more relatable. While it is critical that you are honest in your story, it is also important that you find a way to make your story more compelling, but still accurately reflect your background.

As an interviewer, I see now more than ever that the idea of sharing personal stories that highlight your strengths and character is an extremely effective way for a potential employer to get to know you.

I had a client with a big job on Wall Street who once told me that he didn't think sharing personal anecdotes had anything to do with his job search. I disagreed. This client lived in my neighborhood, and I learned that he had literally helped deliver his baby daughter on the side of the highway during a treacherous snowstorm. The roads were closed, and traffic was at a standstill. They had called the paramedics, but they were also stuck in the snowstorm and couldn't reach them. He and his wife delivered a healthy baby in their car in large part because he was able to rise to the occasion and come through in an emergency.

My client not only showed immense courage, strength, and compassion in this situation, but his personal experience demonstrates that he is someone who can perform well under pressure. The point is if you can deliver a baby in a car, then that tells me or a potential employer that you can "deliver results" under pressure. Weaving this personal story into his narrative will not only ensure that his strengths are highlighted, but also that his story is memorable. He has since pivoted out of Wall Street and is working in the healthcare space in a job that he loves.

Exercise 3: Creating Your Narrative or "Story"

Now that you understand the importance of your story, let's get started on creating it. Answer the questions below to the best of your ability. Think carefully about the path you have traveled and what it means to you. Additionally, focus on which parts of your story highlight your strengths and character and what aspects of your story might be compelling to a future employer. My business partner, Mel, is certified in this wonderful graphic facilitation method from the Grove. With this method you can have a little fun, creating a graphic design with paper and colored markers.

Use the History Timeline shown here to visualize your answers and support your process.

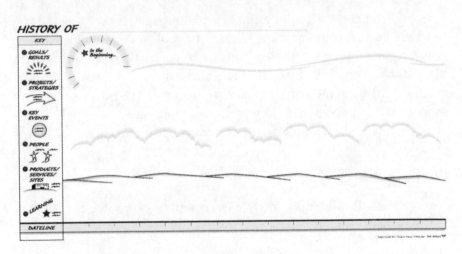

Source: Grove Consultants, Northern California

Let's start at the beginning:

High school (or earlier): What jobs or experiences did you have that led you to your career path?

College:
- Why did you choose to attend a particular college?
- How did you decide on a major or minor?

- Did you change your major?
- Did you attend graduate school?
- What inspired you?
- What were your motivations for making these choices?

For example, since I was the fifth of six kids going through college in my family, my dad gave me a very clear choice. "You can go to any school you want, as long as it's a public university in Illinois!" He told me he was done paying for out-of-state tuition and that was that. My choices became very clear to me from the limited geographical area I had to choose from.

Alternate Path: We all follow different paths, and there is no wrong answer here. If you didn't go to college, that's a part of your story. What was your alternate path when you graduated from high school? College isn't for everyone, so if you went straight to work after high school? Own it and explain it!

Only you know what is best for *you*. Your experiences have led you to where you are today and are relevant to your story. A college degree is not a guarantee or a prerequisite for success. Look at Steve Jobs, Mark Zuckerberg, Bill Gates, and Richard Branson. All really successful and real examples of people who either didn't go to college or dropped out to pursue their dreams. Look at what they accomplished—proving, as I said, that college is not a prerequisite for success!

Employment Experience

Answer the following questions for every single job you've ever had up to the present day:

- What were your job title and responsibilities?
- How did you get the job?
- Did you enjoy your work? In other words, did the work "light you up"?
- If not, what parts do you want to avoid in your next job?
- What new skills did you learn?
- What did you learn about yourself?
- What contributions do you feel you made to the organization and how did those contributions make you feel at the end of the day?

- Why did you leave?
- What other skills would you like to learn in the next job (for your own thought process)?

These answers are for your eyes only. You will use the information to craft your story, and being totally honest with yourself will help you to further zoom in on where you want to go.

There are no wrong answers. Do not judge yourself on where you have been. Honor your path and recognize why you made the decisions that have led you to where you are today. Pay attention to when you listened to your heart and when you were the happiest. Also, notice which of your decisions and experiences led to feeling unhappy or unfulfilled. There is so much to learn from this exercise besides creating a personal narrative, so take your time and answer each question carefully.

Now let's look back at everything you've written:

- What patterns do you see?
- What kind of narrative is emerging?
- Go back to the questions. Where can you go deeper?
- Are there things that you can now answer a little more clearly as you revisit the questions and look at the bigger picture?
- What are you learning about yourself along the way?

Once you have answered the questions above, put an asterisk next to or circle those answers that highlight your strengths or your character the most.

Then do the same for the answers that are most relevant to your current job search. Use the selected answers as the key points to create your narrative. Once you have identified the key points you want to include in your narrative, then weave in personal stories to make it more interesting and compelling.

Next you'll want to practice, practice, practice!

Record yourself telling your story, look in the mirror and tell your story, and do whatever you need to do until you have memorized the points you want to make. Then share your story with your friends or family and ask them what they find the most interesting, compelling, or relevant. Continue to practice this story out loud until it can roll off your tongue naturally and easily in an interview.

You may need to refine or adjust your story from time to time depending on the potential employer you're meeting, but if you put the time in now to make it a compelling and authentic story, it will endure and serve you well for any job search going forward. The goal of storytelling is to highlight your strengths and character, while connecting with the interviewer on a human level and keeping them engaged. I urge you to take your time in developing and practicing this personal narrative, because the story you choose to tell and how you tell it can make all the difference in whether you get the job.

Congratulations! You have now finished another important step on your journey. Give yourself credit for coming this far. Take a breather, take a walk, or take a nap.

For more exercises and exclusive teachings, visit:
MaryOlsonMenzel.com/Resources

Summary

A resume tells. A story sells. A compelling personal narrative is essential to have as you embark on your journey to find your inner light. It illustrates your background and qualities that make you stand out from the rest, which might just put you over the finish line as the best candidate for a role. It is a much more effective way to make a personal connection with a potential employer than a resume alone.

Start at the beginning and be sure to include your twists and turns. Everyone has them! Remember that every experience led you to where you are today. Your story is your opportunity to portray who you are, connect with others, and ultimately land the job of your dreams.

Even if you are not adept at composition or self-promotion, you can still be successful. Record yourself telling your story, recite it in the mirror, or invite friends to listen as you practice it. Continue to do this until your story rolls off your tongue naturally.

4

Build Your Toolbox

"It takes as much energy to wish as it does to plan."

—Eleanor Roosevelt

To GET THE best results in your job search, you should have a well-stocked toolbox, which includes:

- Your authentic light
- Your story
- Your resume
- Your LinkedIn profile and professional brand
- Your network

We discussed how to identify your light in Chapter 2 and then how to develop your story in Chapter 3. In this chapter we discuss two primary concepts: first, how to create an effective resume, and second, how to utilize LinkedIn to boost your job search. Additionally, I will provide tips on how to overcome gaps in your resume if you are reentering the workforce after being out of work or taking a leave of absence. Your trusted network is the final tool in your toolbox. We discuss how to use your personal and professional network to connect with potential employers in some of the following chapters.

Let's move on to the nuts and bolts of every job search.

Your Resume

It is an essential part of your job search to have a clear and concise resume because it is your first written impression for a potential employer and the ticket to getting an interview. It needs to be easy to read, and something that a hiring manager can glance at in an instant and decide whether they want to meet you or not.

Although it varies with the company and the job, on average 500 or more resumes are received for each corporate job opening. If you post your resume online on a major job site like Indeed or LinkedIn so that a recruiter can find it, you are facing stiff competition because as of 2024, there are 225 million resumes on Indeed![1]

When you ask individual recruiters directly, they report that they spend up to five minutes reviewing each resume. However, a recent research study from TheLadder.com that included the direct observation of the actions of corporate recruiters demonstrated that this review time is a huge exaggeration.[2] You may be shocked to know that the average recruiter spends a mere six seconds reviewing a resume. *Six seconds of resume review means recruiters will see very little, so it must stand out!*

Six seconds only allows a recruiter to quickly scan (but not to read) a resume. We also know from observation that nearly four seconds of that six-second scan is spent looking exclusively at four job areas:

- Job titles
- Former/current employers
- Start/end dates of each job
- Education

Like it or not, that narrow focus means that unless you make these four areas extremely easy for them to find within approximately four seconds, the odds are high that you will be instantly passed over.

Also, be aware that whatever else you have on your resume, the recruiter will have only the remaining approximately two seconds to find and be impressed with it. Finally, if you think the information in your cover letter will provide added support for your qualifications, you might be interested to know that not a lot of recruiters bother to even read cover letters at all.

A single resume error can also instantly disqualify you. A shocking 88% of resumes are rejected because of a photo on the resume and according to CV statistics, 76% of CVs are ignored if candidates have an unprofessional email address.[3] Typos and spelling errors are no joke—employers look at that and worry about attention to detail on the job.

In this digital age, if you learn how to optimize your resume for an applicant tracking system, your application doesn't have to be one of the 75% that get rejected before ever landing in front of a human.[4] Research also shows that the format of the resume matters a great deal. Having a clear or professionally organized resume format that presents relevant information where recruiters expect it to be will improve the rating of a resume by a recruiter by a whopping 60% percent, without any change to the content (on a scale of 1–10 this is a 6.2, versus a 3.9 usability rating for the less professionally organized resume). And if you make that common mistake of putting your resume in a PDF format, you should realize that many applicant tracking systems (ATS) will simply not be able to scan and read any part of its content—meaning instant rejection. At this point, the best format for most ATS is Word format.

But please take all of this with a grain of salt, as these parameters are constantly changing regarding what will be picked up by an ATS, and I expect as technology enhancements continue this will become a different story as well.

Weak LinkedIn profiles can also hurt you. We will get to more about this later, but as of the writing of this book, LinkedIn is where the job searchers and the recruiters go most.[5] As of January 2024 there are one billion members and over 58.4 million companies listed on LinkedIn, with more than 15 million open job listings (LinkedIn). These figures make it no surprise to learn that 72% of recruiters use or engage LinkedIn at some point in their recruitment process.

And, because many recruiters and hiring managers use LinkedIn profiles either to verify or to supplement resume information, those profiles also impact your chances of getting noticed in a positive way. Recruiters spend an average of 19% of their time on your LinkedIn profile simply looking at your activity and viewing your picture (so a professional picture is a must).[6] The research also revealed that just like resumes, weak organization and "scanability" within a LinkedIn profile negatively impacted the recruiter's ability to "process the profile."[7]

Other relevant facts:

- The job search: Up to 80% of job searches are found through networking, according to a report from ABC News.
- 94% of recruiters use social media for recruiting. This number has increased steadily for the last 10 years.
- Employers who used social media to hire found a 49% improvement in candidate quality over candidates sourced only through traditional recruiting channels, according to Jobvite.
- 96% of workers are looking for a new job in 2023.[8]

In the digital and mobile age of application tracking systems, the right keywords are necessary for recruiters to find something specific in a search. This is called SEO (search engine optimization). One of the perks of AI is that this has become easier. Here are some great links for you to learn more about what this is and how to properly get it done, and keep in mind that as technology advances, this will change too!

According to *Forbes* magazine, the best resume writing company that is affordable, offers high-quality review and writing services, and is easy to use is TopResume. This site provides the professionalism and quality most mid- to high-level job seekers need, from its free resume review to its customizable options. (https://www.forbes.com/sites/forbes-personal-shopper/article/best-resume-writing-services).

Other options include: **https://enhancv.com/, https://resume genius.com/rg/brilliant-resume-builder**, and **https://www.grammarly .com/**.

If your resume is clear and concise, looks interesting and worth a second look, hiring managers or recruiters will typically go straight to your LinkedIn profile to take a deeper and more in-depth look at who you are.

Your LinkedIn Profile

Your digital profile matters. As mentioned, in today's professional arena, it is imperative that you have a professional LinkedIn profile. Not only is it an opportunity to get noticed, but it is currently one of the most effective sources for connecting with potential employers, sharing news, nurturing and expanding your network, and ultimately finding a job.

LinkedIn has been growing as a professional network since 2003 and is connecting more and more people every day. While a resume is a summary of your career history, the LinkedIn profile provides a more complete picture of you as a professional and what you care about—*your professional brand*. Beyond a resume, your LinkedIn profile shows your connections, your depth of network, and what people are saying about you, which is extraordinarily helpful to someone who is considering offering you a job. Before I go into any meeting or hop on a call with any executive, I will go to their LinkedIn profile to learn more, to see if we have any mutual connections, and to read the recommendations to get an idea of who they are.

When searching for a job or building your professional brand, LinkedIn should be your new "best friend" and as of 2024, one of the best online resources for your job search endeavors. I tell my clients to follow every company and person that they would like to connect with on LinkedIn. Since you can customize your LinkedIn profile to meet your specific interests, I advise my clients to log into LinkedIn every morning over their coffee or tea and to read the newsfeed of all the companies and people that they are following. This is a great place for you to keep your finger on the pulse of your professional network and job search and also discover what is going on out there in the business world.

Here are a few of the best expert recommendations straight from LinkedIn for learning how to build your profile:

- **Add a professional photo.** You're 14 times more likely to be viewed if you have a photo.
- **Write an attention-grabbing headline.** Explain what it is you do. Show your passion and value.
- **Draft a compelling summary.** Focus on career accomplishments in 40 words or more. Include keywords but not buzzwords.
- **Detail your past work experience.** You're 12 times more likely to be viewed if you have more than one position listed.
- **Add skills and get endorsements.** Include a mix of high-level and niche skills.
- **Include volunteer experiences and causes.** Almost half of all hiring managers say they view them as equivalent to formal work.

If you have been out of work for a while and have a career gap in your resume or LinkedIn profile, it is not necessarily a deal breaker for employers anymore. If the gap between jobs is more than a year, most employers will ask why, so be prepared to tell your story. Don't stress. Be honest and get creative about what you have been doing and how those skills can translate into a new role. Think about how best to present the story of your life in between jobs. Did you step out of the workforce to raise children, take care of an elderly parent, write a book, travel the world, or do charity work?

Whatever the reason, it has become perfectly acceptable to step out of the workforce and hit the pause button. Just be prepared to discuss the choices you made and why. When you tell the story of your decision to leave the workforce, focus on what you did or accomplished during that time. This can illustrate that you either maintained existing skills, learned new skills, or gained other experiences or perspectives that contribute to your value, or which are relevant to a potential employer. As we discussed in Chapter 3, a well-told story not only makes you more memorable but is also more likely to resonate with a potential employer.

For example, one of my clients explained her five-year career gap by saying she had been the chief operating officer of her household—raising kids, volunteering at schools, and keeping the home fires burning. This was a creative way to explain the truth about what she had been up to since the last time she was gainfully employed. She recognized that even if she wasn't being paid, her contributions had value and meaning. She was an organizer, a therapist, a fundraiser, a chef, a chauffeur, and an administrator all wrapped up into one job.

Another client and friend listed her job title as "Head of Management and Logistics for the Collins Family." Well done, Lisa—both creative and true!

I also really liked something that another woman, who is currently the head of human resources for one of our client companies, put on her LinkedIn profile. While she was in transition with her current role, she wrote as her headline: "Coming Soon—to be announced." This was a brilliant, honest, and bold way to describe her search and pique some curiosity for her viewers in between jobs and during her job search.

However, when you do choose to list your employment gap on your resume or LinkedIn profile, your goal is to show a potential employer that the talents and skills that you exhibited during this time are of value to their organization. We all have a story, which includes the ups and downs and decisions/choices made from either necessity or desire. Telling your story as honestly and authentically as possible helps demonstrate to a future employer that you are someone they can trust.

Our world has changed so much and continues to evolve in ways we could have never imagined. During the Covid-19 pandemic, we were all in the same "storm," but we were not necessarily in the same "boat." Our home situations may have been different, but we all did the best we could at that moment in time. The pandemic has completely changed the way many employers look at work and life. We have all been humanized in a way that creates more empathy for whatever boat you're in. So keep the story real and truthful. Letting your authenticity and values shine through will demonstrate that you are someone with integrity and worthy of a second look despite your employment gap.

Just remember, a gap in your career history does not change the fact that you have skills, qualities, and talents to offer to an employer that go above and beyond your experience.

Employers are always looking for:

- Creativity
- Clear communication skills
- Collaboration
- Quick, analytical thinking
- Organizational skills
- Intelligence (emotional and intellectual)
- Flexibility/adaptability
- Quick learning
- Resilience
- Problem-solving skills
- Enthusiasm

As a result, I recommend that you find ways to highlight that you utilized these important skills during your leave of absence no matter what you did in between jobs.

Your resume and your LinkedIn profile are two important components of your job search toolbox, which not only summarize your experience but also illustrate what you bring to the table and explain how your skills and experience can meet future employers' needs.

Summary

Now that you've identified your light and your story, it's time to turn your attention to two more assets in your toolbox: your resume and your LinkedIn profile.

Your clear and concise resume is your ticket to getting noticed among all the many other candidates out there. It is often a potential employer's first impression of you and, since it's not considered for more than a few minutes at most, it must be captivating. A single error on your resume can disqualify you from consideration for a job.

Weak LinkedIn profiles can also hurt you. Not only is it necessary to have a LinkedIn profile, but also it's important that you have an impressive one. Before I go into any meeting with an executive, I will check their LinkedIn profile to review their professional history, see if we have common connections, and generally learn more about the person with whom I'm meeting.

On LinkedIn, your photo, your headline, your summary, your past work experience, and what people are saying about you will all be scrutinized. Take the right steps to make it a good representation of your professional brand.

5

Follow Your Dream

"Whatever you can do, or dream you can do, begin it. Boldness and action has genius, magic, grace and power in it."

—Johann Wolfgang von Goethe

I HOPE THAT by reading this book you are starting to feel more energized and lit up by the possibilities ahead. I hope that you are beginning to let some of your insecurities dissolve about what you can or can't do. In the classes I offer and with the clients I coach, this is the point in the process where people start to recognize their value and the true strengths that they have had all along. Realizing that you already have what you need to be great and land your dream job is exciting and empowering all at once.

Not quite feeling it yet? That's okay, too. Keep going.

Don't give up before the magic sets in.

Looking for a job is a job unto itself; it takes energy, focus, and strategy. In this chapter, we will be working on building your career, not just finding you a job. Our goal is to build a career that gets your head off the pillow each day excited for what the day will bring, a career that reignites your inner light. So many people settle for what's in front of them. Not you. Not anymore. Because you are reading and working through this book, you've made it clear that you desire more, and I think you deserve more, too.

Realizing that you already have what you need to be great is truly eye-opening and exciting. You can do this!

Let's look back at my friend, Ken, from the Tribune Company. Because of his energy and his light, sales were up, the team was energized, and the CEO who hired him couldn't have been happier. Ken knew that the odds were stacked against him, and yet one day he said, "I can do this." He walked across the street and into the offices of his main competitor in town and said, "I'm here, I have the skills and lots of energy, and you should hire me!" He had nothing to lose. He did not have the perfect pedigree, but he had a bright inner light, belief in his abilities, and perseverance. He got bold and broke through the mold. He not only got hired but he got promoted, again and again.

According to a 2023 Pew Research Center survey, about half of workers are highly satisfied with their job overall.[1] However, I'd estimate that about 70% of the workforce is not fully "lit up." They are doing jobs they think they should do, not what they dream of doing. Maybe they followed the dreams that their parents had for them but were never quite happy in their work.

We all know the saying "Life is short," but a long day at the office feels like an eternity if you are not doing something you love. On the flipside, when you're engrossed in doing something you love, time flies.

I never want you to feel stuck. You can always change your mind, no matter what stage you're at in your career. Following your instincts and doing what makes you happy in your work is the goal. You should always aim to make a difference doing something that matters to you. It's okay to pivot, perhaps even more than once. I did. And I'm giving you permission right now to usher in a new way of working, which may make you feel uncomfortable at times, but it will pass. Pushing yourself outside of your comfort zone is the best way to grow. Say yes to what is calling you and you will never regret it.

We hired a college student, Kate, who babysat for me when our kids were younger and I was working. She was a finance major in the middle of a financial services internship and was really unhappy. We sat down on my couch and as she cried about this, I told her, "Follow your passions *now*. I care about you and don't want you to wake up when you're 40, feeling like you followed the wrong path." We created a plan to help her pivot out of finance and into what she loved. She wanted to get involved in sustainable farming, as she was very passionate about being a vegan. We found her an amazing job working for an organic, healthy food delivery company called Sakara, and I'm happy to say she has been there for four years, and she just got another promotion. I'm so glad I was able to help her find what lights her up and makes her heart sing.

Don't wait until you think you're ready. Do it now—there's no time like the present to dream a new dream and create an actionable plan to make it a reality.

Recently, a potential client who was asking about our coaching services during a Zoom call said to me, "I really want to hire you but I'm not ready yet because I don't have enough clarity about what I want to do next." This executive was a VP of communications for a major company. I smiled at him on the computer screen and said, "This is *exactly* why you need us! If clarity and direction are what you're looking for, we can help you."

We often don't know exactly what we need, and it's okay not to know. Sometimes we're simply too close to it, and not clearly seeing what our options are in the moment. Not knowing is a great beginning. In my firm, we help people see the direction that opens them up to new possibilities. The next day we got an email from that client saying, "I'm ready—when do we start?" Since then, he has followed through on everything he wanted and asked for an expanded role at his current company and is knocking it out of the park! He's now feeling challenged and appreciated and has a bigger team to help him get more of the important things done to live his dream.

The beautiful thing about exploring your own life, your specific wants, and desires for your future is that there are no limits. The only limits are those that you put upon yourself. No matter your circumstances, if you want to change your life for the better, it's up to you. At each career stage and life stage, what you want will look slightly different. The process of defining what you want is the same but the stakes can be very different. Early in your career, you have different needs than when starting a family or devising your exit plan for retirement. You alone will know what's most important for you at each life stage, and I suggest making a checklist of what you need at each stage.

In my opinion, *now* is always the best time to explore what you want from this precious life. Why put off making decisions that will affect your life and your future for the better? The pandemic, the great resignation, layoffs, quiet quitting, quiet hiring, political unrest, and wars—all are factors that influence how we look at work. Every year brings something new and what we go through teaches us so much about how, where, and what we need to thrive in our work and life, despite what's going on around us. The rules of work as we used to know them have changed greatly and even our geographical boundaries have shifted. With all these shifts comes the opportunity to be more creative and intentional as we move forward.

Your next career adventure awaits you! It can be either at your own organization or somewhere else. Your career is in your hands, and you have to take that responsibility and own it.

How can you discover or uncover your gifts and strengths? As seasoned executives, many of us are familiar with our strengths and weaknesses, but it never hurts to take a deeper dive and rediscover what it is that truly lights us up. Also, you may be at a point where you have just been doing the same thing for so long that you want to remember what you love.

There is a wonderful tool called StrengthsFinder 2.0.[2] You can order the book on Amazon, Barnes and Noble or go to the website to take the assessment for a small fee. It will identify your top five strengths and how you can develop and apply them to your work and personal life.

Once you have identified your strengths and have begun paying attention to what it is that lights you up, you can start to create more opportunities to use these strengths in your day-to-day work. You can begin to look around for the things that will help elevate your natural gifts at your own organization. There are more tools at your fingertips than you think; you just have to look for them. Most companies also have a learning and development team that can offer you specific programs.

How do you balance following your purpose or passion with your financial needs and goals? As I mentioned earlier, at each life stage the stakes are different, and so is our need for achieving our highest earning potential. Purpose and passion matter, but so does your need to pay the bills. Truly, only you can discern when it may be right to take a pay cut to follow your dreams. Thus, it's important to weigh out each choice carefully based on where you are in life and what you need not only to survive but to thrive.

Overall, when you're in touch with who you are and intentional about your career, it's easier to identify and go for the jobs and situations that will light you up daily. When you know what you want from your career, it becomes easier to design a life that checks most of the boxes that you need and want to make it fulfilling and fun.

Be deliberate, and keep creating your plan and strategy to get to where you want to be in life. Keep tweaking and adjusting as your needs and desires change. Be patient with yourself and the process as it unfolds. Life is a journey, and when you follow your heart toward what it is that truly lights you up, you cannot go wrong. You have to be strategic in this process. When you create a vision and a deliberate plan about your career and your future and make decisions based on truly knowing yourself, you're headed in the right direction. When you know who you are, what you bring to the table, and what you want, you can gain the important insights to design your path with greater clarity and conviction.

Start now. Day by day. Step by step (even if they're baby steps!). Each day is a new opportunity to get it right.

Summary

This is the point in the process in which people typically begin to recognize their value and true strengths that they've had all along. If you're not one of those people, keep going. Don't give up before the magic sets in. Looking for a new job is difficult enough. You're working toward building your new career and that can be a full-time job in itself, but one that is certainly worth doing.

I estimate that about 70% of the workforce is not fully "lit up" and I don't want that to be you, ever again. I never want you to feel stuck and I urge you to change your mind if you have to, at any point in your career. I did more than once and I'm giving you permission to usher in a new way of thinking about your career and working. Say yes to what's calling you. The only limit to truly exploring your desires for your future is what you impose on yourself.

Understanding your own needs and non-negotiables in order to make it through every different life stage is necessary during this time of exploration. At each life stage the stakes are different, and so is our need for achieving our highest earning potential. Purpose and passion matter, but so does your need to pay the bills. Thus, it's important to weigh out each choice carefully based on where you are in life and what you need not only to survive but to thrive.

6

Tap into Your Network

"Life's most persistent and urgent question is: What are you doing for others?"
—Martin Luther King, Jr.

THE SIMPLE QUESTION "How can I help?" is one that so many people forget to ask and then end up missing out on a very powerful opportunity for connection. It's a question that reaches people's hearts and minds with compassion. Genuine compassion in any scenario has the power to light others up.

When the pandemic hit in March 2020, I called an MVP team meeting and said, "We need to call every client and ask how we can help them." This has made all the difference in how our company has weathered and thrived during the pandemic and well beyond.

In almost every single meeting I have, I ask, "What can I do to help you? Essentially, how can I use my expertise to make your life better or easier?" This question often disarms people. When you come from a place of truly wanting to help, you'd be surprised at the reactions and the results that follow after asking this question.

Offering to Help

We live in a world where so many people think of things in terms of "What's in it for me?" I believe this is backward. The questions we should all be asking are these:

- How can we make each other better?
- How can we help each other rise to even greater success by offering up our skills and talents to work together toward the common goal of success?
- How can I make your life easier?

One client makes me smile every time I think of him. Larry and I were working together on his next career pivot, doing a lot of the exercises you're doing in this book. He was in the thick of interviewing with quite a few amazing companies. We were analyzing the potential opportunities when all the positions were put on hold due to the uncertainty of the marketplace during the pandemic. It was at the beginning of March 2020 and businesses were shutting down; no one knew what was coming next, and everyone was in a panic. I suggested that Larry take care of himself and his family first and then think of the companies with whom he was in the middle of interviewing. I asked him to identify which company he most wanted to work for based on the list we had made. He was very clear that it was a certain tech company in Silicon Valley. Then I said, "Call that company today and ask the CEO, 'How can I help at this time? I realize that you might need someone to lead through this time from a financial perspective. I'm a CFO and I can help you now to navigate your finance department. What do you need today while you're waiting to make a permanent hiring decision? What can I do to help take the pressure off you as a CEO?'"

He did this and the CEO was taken aback. He wondered, who is this person who cares enough to ask this question and is so willing to help before he's even offered a job? This simple question impressed the CEO greatly, and he thanked my client for asking, saying he'd get back to him shortly. The CEO called back several days later and offered my client an unexpected consulting gig immediately with the additional promise that if things went well, they could talk about the full-time CFO role.

This is an example of a real person asking a real question and offering to help, which changed his career trajectory and the entire experience for both parties. Larry is still there years later, extremely happy and thriving.

During a global crisis of any sort, there can be a feeling of just needing to stay where you are for the moment, to play it safe. A lot of people put their job searches on hold in 2020. In the example above, my client could have shrugged his shoulders and put his job search on hold, too, while the world shut down, or even given up altogether. But he didn't. Instead, he asked where and how he could be of service to a fellow human being during a time of fear and uncertainty. This simple question eventually led him to a job offer. This is also an example of how a little coaching and guidance can pay off in huge ways.

Couldn't we all use a little help here and there as we navigate through the twists and turns of our lives? Embracing the mentality of helping others and wanting to make a difference is an attitude that will bring opportunities your way. Companies want to hire people who are interested in helping to find solutions.

"How can I help?" is such a simple question, but one that illustrates not only compassion but also the motivation to act, which is exactly what employers are looking for. This way of thinking transfers you right into the next section and will help you to find the best way to tap into your network for help, too!

If your light is your innate superpower, then your network is the superhighway that will help you get to where you want to go. Networks and referrals can be the most important source for your next career move. This is your chance to stand out in the crowd based on "who you know", not only what you know. More than ever, your professional network is like a precious gift to tend to and care for regularly, at every stage of your career.

I have been advising my clients for years to make sure that they are checking in with their network on a regular basis. Especially now, as our world continues to shift in so many different ways, it's a very organic thing to check in and see how they've been doing and managing through all of the changes in the work world and beyond. Everyone appreciates a genuine and caring check-in. It must be authentic. Practice bringing your light to others, ask how you can help them, and see what unfolds—for you both. Take the attention off yourself as you are reaching out and let the exchange come from a genuine place of caring. The more you practice connecting with your network, the more it becomes natural and the more you will enjoy it. Exchanging good energy is invigorating and can spark new ideas. It's purposeful and cre-ates pathways to the unexpected blessings of a natural and organic connection.

With these natural and organic connections, you are building or deepening a relationship, getting to know each other, and finding mutually beneficial ways to connect on a human level. It's an invest-ment in time, and worth every minute. Don't rush it. Make it real. If you're looking for a job, make it your goal to check in with at least one person in your network per day. Daily practices like this, in addition to reading your LinkedIn newsfeed, will become healthy habits that keep you up to speed with what's happening out there with the people and the industries that you're interested in. It will also remind you that you are not alone. Become a student of life and stay connected and abreast of all that's happening so that you can speak intelligently to anyone in your network.

Asking for Help

Everyone needs help, even the most successful people you know did not get to where they are without a team of people helping them, so don't be afraid to ask for it when needed. Asking for help in the right way and at the right time is just as powerful as asking, "How can I help?" Once a connection is made, it starts to unfold as a relationship. Be clear in identifying the help you need. Gather your thoughts and let yourself breathe into the question. People want to help, and often you'll create a win-win situation where you can help one another, maybe not always right away, but down the road. This is the power of your connections.

When someone asks how they can help you, be prepared to answer with specifics:

- Do you need contacts at a certain company?
- Do you need someone to help you with technology?
- Do you need a coach or a mentor?
- Do you need a referral to podcasts or books that supply contin-ued inspiration and education?
- Do you need help amplifying your business or product?

Most people are open and willing to help if they can and will happily make an introduction for you to someone else in their network. Keep asking the questions and don't be afraid to lean in for a little help from your network and your friends. The more people you can speak to, the more thoughts, ideas, and advice you'll get. These conversations will start to point you in the right direction.

At the end of the day, we're all looking for reciprocal relationships, so practice asking what you can do to help the people with whom you're meeting. You might think there's nothing you can do to help them but you never know until you ask! Whether it's business-related or personal, maybe they can connect you to a company you've always wanted to work for and you can get them great theater tickets, baseball tickets, or help their kids on the soccer team.

Most likely, it's the people in your network who will be the ones to help you find your next position. And those are the people you trust and who will represent you in a positive light to potential future employers. When talking with people, it's okay to say, "Who else can you connect me with?" Ask and you may receive in ways that could change your path for the better.

Working with Recruiters

I'd be remiss if I didn't mention the importance of recruiters. They are also an integral piece of this puzzle and an amazing resource for you in your hunt for the next job. As a former recruiter, I can tell you there is great value in having deep relationships with recruiters and search firms. Some of the people I have hired and placed with various companies have become dear friends who are an important part of my network.

When I was running executive search and deep into my recruiting career, I would get asked, "How do I hire you to be *my* recruiter?" As much as I wanted to help everyone I met and be their personal "talent agent," the world of recruiting just doesn't work that way. If you want to hire someone who can help you position yourself to find your next job, you can hire someone like me or another coach from MVP—or a career coach and pay them a fee. Most recruiters are hired by the client to find people to fill a specific position in a company, not hired by an individual looking for a job.

So it's important to be aware of the different types of recruiters and how you can work with them. The three main types of recruiting firms are categorized as staffing firms, contingency recruiting firms, and retained recruiting firms. The next sections explain each of these.

Staffing Firms

A staffing firm hires individuals for a client company's temporary or contract needs. In this type of firm, the candidate is actually employed by the staffing firm, which is then responsible for paying all salaries, taxes, and sometimes benefits. Many times the staffing firm has options in the contract for the employer to hire the employee after a certain amount of time. The client pays an hourly rate for the contract employee, and this rate also includes the fee for the staffing firm. The candidate does not pay anything out of pocket for this service.

Contingency Recruiting Firms

A contingency recruiting firm does a specific search on a contingency basis for a specified role for a company, such as an accountant, a technology expert, or a sales executive. The recruiter is *only* paid upon a successful placement. They do all of the initial outreach, screening and interviewing and then they work with the hiring manager to set up interviews for the client company. The company typically pays a 25% fee of the employee's estimated first year's compensation package. Once again, the candidate does not pay a fee for this; only the client pays.

Retained Recruiting Firms

A retained recruiting firm is at the higher end. The biggest difference between a contingency and a retained firm is that the client company pays a retainer fee to have that company perform a search. Typically this is a 33% fee, paid out in thirds: one-third at the time of engagement, one-third halfway through the search, and one-third upon offer. The initial retainer fee is paid whether or not a hire is made. Companies use retained search firms for higher-level positions, ranging from director level to CEO, typically in a salary range of $200,000 and higher.

In addition to these three types, there are now firms that are using the term "container," which, due to client needs and demand, is a hybrid of both contingency and retained. And I'm sure it will keep evolving!

So the reality is that recruiters are really working for the client company, not for you. That being said, it's still in your best interest to develop relationships with at least a few recruiters you can trust and hope that they keep you in mind as positions from clients come across their desks. Most good recruiters are relationship builders and want to get to know you before an open position crosses their desk. You never know where it will lead, for either the recruiter or the candidate. Stay in touch and keep the recruiters updated on your employment status and desires for your next role. This way, if the recruiter has a client need that fits your skill set, you'll hear about it.

Schedule informational coffee meetings to meet and expand your network, either in person or on Zoom. Put yourself out there! Try to find a way to make it to professional networking breakfasts, luncheons, and cocktail events. You can even go with a friend if you need to; it's less daunting. Try to walk away from each meeting with three new names to add to your network. Stay current with, expand, and enhance the quality of your network.

Making Contact

Following are some sample letters for different scenarios you can use for inspiration. But please, use your own voice and style in every communication!

Dear _____,

I hope this email finds you well. My name is _____ and I am currently exploring my next career adventure. Your company is among the top on my target list. You may notice that we are connected by _____ on LinkedIn. _____ and I know each other from _____. I'd be so appreciative of any advice you may offer or guidance that you may be able to provide to me as I work towards my next role. Learning from you would be a great opportunity. I would, of course, pay forward your generosity in the future.

I hope to hear back from you soon and have the chance to meet and learn more about how I may fit at a company like _____.

My very best,

Dear _____,

I hope this email finds you well. My name is _____ and I am interested in learning more about your organization/industry/role, particularly how you were able to achieve your success. I'm in the process of securing my next position and would really value a conversation with you as I work towards my next role. Could I offer to buy you a cup of coffee so that we can chat? You'll notice that we are both connected to _____ on LinkedIn. _____ and I know each other from _____. I'd love to hear about how you both met.

Best,

Dear _____,

I hope this note finds you well. I'm currently exploring my next business adventure and would like to see if you are open to a meeting. We are connected by _____ on LinkedIn and they are _____ in relation to my work. I would greatly appreciate it if we could set up either an in-person or a virtual coffee in order to learn more about you and your business and to see if we can find a way to help each other.

Please let me know how the next few weeks work for you.

Thank you in advance for your help!

Best regards,

This step can be uncomfortable for some, especially those who are introverted. Embrace the uncomfortable feeling and move through it. You'll get more comfortable once you start to experience positive connections and meetings with people who want to help you. And for the extroverted and born networkers out there, it's an exhilarating adventure! Either way, it's an integral step in the process of finding a job that lights you up, so you might as well embrace it.

When trying to schedule a meeting with a "friend of a friend" try to meet them in person if you can, but if that's not possible, a Zoom meeting will suffice. Keep in mind that most people are extremely busy, so asking for a quick 20 minutes makes it easy for them to meet with you. Offer to come to their offices or meet at a venue of their choice. When 20 minutes have passed, offer to let them go—don't overstay your welcome with someone who is doing you a favor. If it turns into a longer meeting, then that's a bonus!

Be confident and authentic in your own light. Quiet confidence—which I will delve into in more detail soon, is the inner knowing that you are worth something to a potential employer—is so important. If your friends and the people in your network sense your self-confidence and your integrity, they will be happy to connect you with others. Always offer to return the favor and to work with integrity and honesty as you represent yourself to potential future employers.

Be thoughtful in your follow-up and leave a lasting impression with those you meet by sending an email immediately following your meeting and a handwritten note within a week after. You can always follow up again and stay top of mind a few weeks after your meeting as well. Just remember that there is a fine line between being persistent and being annoying.

Make sure that your connections are high quality and mutually beneficial. Having meaningful conversations about what the possibilities are is eye-opening and educational. Think of it as a chance not only to gather industry knowledge, but also to market yourself and leave a lasting positive impression. Connections can take you down paths that you never even knew existed. There is great potential and opportunity with every person you connect with. These people will become business connections that could turn into friendships that will last far into the future, even after you've landed that "dream job"!

Summary

Genuine compassion in any scenario has the power to light others up. Consider not what's in it for you, but how you can help others. The goal is to rise to even greater success by offering up our skills and talents to work together toward the common goal of success for ourselves and others. We are all better together. And while many people are living in the reverse, this is just one more thing that can help you stand out among the crowd, enhance your light, and also bring out others' inner light in the process.

If you're looking for a job, make it a goal to check in with at least one person in your network per day. Regularly read your LinkedIn newsfeed. These things will both enhance your network and remind you that you are not alone. Once you make a habit of this, you'll see that asking for help in the right way is just as powerful as asking "How can I help?" Reciprocal relationships are the goal of building a network and often the people in your network will be the ones to help you find your next position.

Put yourself out there to build your network, even if it feels less than comfortable. Whether or not you love connecting with strangers in your professional life, be confident, authentic, and thoughtful. Always remember to follow up with a note of thanks. Having meaningful conversations about what the possibilities are is eye-opening and educational. Think of it as a chance not only to gather industry knowledge, but to market yourself and leave a lasting positive impression.

7

Choose Joy

"Money is only a tool. It will take you wherever you wish, but it will not replace you as the driver."

—Ayn Rand

WE ARE ALL navigating the realities of our life situations. You do have to work, and I want you to live with your light on, but how do you do that if you're unhappy in your job, or feel like you're short changing your career?

If you feel like you're not getting an equitable trade for your paycheck, you could turn resentful, and that can affect not only your work but your health, your family, and your life. You could also impact everyone else you work with. Don't think you're fooling anyone; people can see it. I see it often with clients who come to me feeling stuck, asking me to help them get "unstuck."

If you're lucky enough, you may have "fallen into a great career" by accident, or a great job just "fell into your lap." Most likely the reality is that it didn't just fall into your lap, but you were open to the opportunity when it presented itself to you. The fact is opportunities only fall into your lap when you are open to seeing them. If you're walking through life with blinders on, you might not even recognize the opportunity in front of you.

As I mentioned earlier, I "fell" into recruiting at a young age because I was so open. My first job out of college was as a television reporter. I was driven by the story, driven by what made people tick. I couldn't see then how this job was a perfect step for what came next. I was driven by the people and their stories and what lit them up from the inside out.

I hit my first career crossroads at the age of 23, when I realized that my next career move was to a small town away from my family and friends. I didn't want to move. I wanted to stay in Chicago near my family and friends and my fiancé, Kurt.

I answered an ad in the *Chicago Tribune* (which would much later become my favorite place of employment), put on my favorite suit from Lord & Taylor, and went to interview at a search firm in Oak Brook, Illinois. What happened next, you might say, is that an opportunity fell into my lap, because I was open to it! After meeting with the principal, he asked me if I would be open to meeting more people at the firm. He thought I had great potential as a recruiter and a salesperson. I didn't really know what being a recruiter entailed, but I did know that I loved interviewing people and finding out what drives them to be who they are and to do what they do. From an early age, I had an intuitive sense of people and discerning what they were all about.

I recently worked with a woman who had a great career working for a major brand for 25 years. However, with the placement of a new boss who did not share her vision or values, she felt lost. I could see it in her eyes—she felt defeated and was starting to lose her confidence. She didn't know what to do or where to go, so she came to us for help.

Here's how it went down:

- She concluded and accepted that she needed a change.
- She faced the fact that she didn't know where to begin. (None of us do until we get started. That's why you bought this book!)
- She had the courage to ask for help, so she hired us to be her coaches.
- She revisited her priorities and addressed them in a holistic manner to help her find the right job for her life right now.
- She started following the same process outlined in this book.
- She gained new confidence and courage to go after the jobs that she wanted.

- She got a new job at a smaller, very different kind of company where she can have a greater impact. It's exciting to her.
- The role was one that surprised us both, but one that was uncovered as we went through the process.

When you stop shortchanging yourself, things that you never knew were possible suddenly become possible and it's a beautiful unfolding that no one can predict when you start.

Similarly, there are times when the road you are traveling on and enjoying gives you an unexpected detour. Don't be afraid to take it. It could help you more than you know; it could be the path that sets you up for the rest of your life.

It happened to me in 2003. Fresh out of business school with my newly framed MBA from Northwestern's Kellogg School of Business, I left the corporate offices and a job I loved in the hallowed halls of the Tribune Tower and did a three-year stint at WGN-TV in ad sales. I was excited yet scared. This detour would teach me incredible skills and insights about the inner workings of a sales executive at a television station and because of that, later in my career, I was able to help guide high-performing sales people into future successes.

The problem was that I knew quite early on that my heart wasn't in it and my light wasn't shining. However, through those years, I gained great hands-on experience that I could not have learned in any textbook and made a few amazing friends there too! When I walked into WGN from the corporate offices with my pearls and my blue suit, it was like walking into the Wild West—so very different from what I was used to. I went from the magic of global strategy and leadership at business school to finding myself in a cubicle trying to learn how to build an Excel spreadsheet and do media math. I was a fish out of water, and it was hard for me. At times I cried on my way to work, but I did not give up. I showed up and did my best.

Throughout those years, I had frequent sinus infections and illnesses and my health suffered. My heart and my work were not in sync, and I knew it in my gut—my body was telling me quite loudly. To this day, I am grateful for the leaders of WGN who had such patience with me to teach and help the "kid from corporate." But I knew it wasn't the right long-term fit for me—and I'm pretty sure they knew it, too. Either way, I learned a ton and it was an extremely valuable experience overall.

Every experience you have is the perfect preparation for your future. So find the gift in each situation, learn what you can from it, and take it with you to your next adventure.

After that experience, I was much clearer about what I wanted to do next. I dusted off my pearls and went back to recruiting and coaching. I was back in my happy place and my work had more meaning for me again. From there my work continued to evolve, and I was given more and more responsibilities. My health improved, too.

We are all human. Life is not always perfect. Sometimes your light will dim, and then go on and maybe even off for a time, and that's okay. It happens to us all.

A few years ago, I was bogged down with the administrative tasks of running my business post-Covid, and my son, Christopher, stopped me and asked, "Mom, does your job still light you up?" He knew I was writing a book about this, and had heard me coaching a multitude of clients about doing what they love. His question literally stopped me in my tracks. I paused for a moment to think about his question. At that very juncture, it did not light me up. I was very stressed, stretched too thin, and bogged down with administrative work that I didn't like and was not good at. I had too much responsibility and too much on my plate. It felt like I had the weight of the world on my shoulders, and my sweet son saw it, even before I did.

My son pays attention and knows what I do for a living, and he sees and hears me motivating my clients left and right. I had to look into his earnest big brown eyes and answer honestly. So I took a deep breath and said, "Most of the time it does, but not today, honey." He shrugged his shoulders and said, "Well, you certainly don't seem 'lit up.' You need to get back to that positive energy, Mom. The world needs you." What a wise young soul!

I had to stand in my truth and had no choice but to reassess what I was doing and start thinking about delegating more to my team. I had to ask for help, and that wasn't easy for me. I would have probably gone on like this for a while, lost in my own stuff, but Christopher was astute enough to point it out to me before it went too far. Our kids, our family, and those we love are the ones who can reflect back to us what we cannot always see.

People can see it when you're not lit up, and it affects everyone around you. You cannot hide from this, no matter how brightly you are used to shining. My 11-year-old saw it immediately and I am grateful to him for pointing it out.

Your skills + Your light + Your passion + Your energy = Paycheck! Onward you go!

Summary

You must be open to and ready for opportunities in order to succeed. You never know when the next great thing will offer itself to you. If you're walking through life with blinders on, you might not even recognize the opportunity in front of you.

Sometimes the opportunity ahead looks more like a detour. If that's the case, don't be afraid to take it because it could be the opportunity that sets you up for success for the rest of your life. It happened to me. It's happened to my clients. Sometimes your light has to dim, and then go on and maybe even off for a time, and that's okay. Continue your journey toward joy. It will all lead to where you are meant to be.

8

Develop Your Three Ps

"Just go after your wish. As soon as you start to pursue a dream, your life wakes up and everything has meaning."

—Barbara Sher

THIS IS ONE *of my favorite parts of the process and one that will help you to become very strategic, intentional, and proactive about your job search. With this approach, you will not be waiting around for a position to open, or scouring the job openings online praying for a match as one would do in a traditional job search. Instead, you will create a list that will target exactly which company you would like to work for. Essentially, you are flipping your job search inside out.*

Here is where the magic starts to take shape and you begin to design your future and act in a way that will direct you right towards the results that you are looking for.

Let's dive in! Take out your trusted notebook, and you can also use the worksheets in the back of this book. The first step as you start to think about creating the target list of companies that *you* are interested in is to keep an open mind and to cast a wide net. Write down *every* company you can think of that you might want to work for and keep going, make it as robust as possible, and you will narrow it down later as you gather more information about each organization.

On this list, you will start to identify companies or organizations that you may have admired for a while or that you may have recently found intriguing online or in a conversation. This process will involve a fair amount of research to determine which companies you are connected to, people you are connected to, and organizations that are worth pursuing. Also, begin to think about and research which companies might be the right cultural fit for you. It takes some time, but it's worth the effort, especially as you start to see things unfold.

This is the game changer where you get to act, gain positive momentum, and put into play all of the things you have been working on thus far! Take your time and have some fun with this; it's a research project that will begin to put you onto a new trajectory for your future. As you populate this list of companies, you will see that once the list is in place and you start having conversations, you will be able to envision a whole new world of potential.

This target list will also set you up to have conversations with the right people in the right places, even before there is a job opening, thus being ahead of the game. *This is key: you want to be connected even before there is an opening and build relationships with people at these organizations as a part of your trusted network.* That way, once you're connected in a meaningful way, you have the potential to be top of mind when the "perfect" job opens. For one of my clients, the company liked her so much that when they connected with her, they created a role for her. It was a role that they had been thinking about for some time and when she walked in the door, they realized that someone with her background was exactly what they wanted. It's not the norm, but it is great timing when an organization's need coincides with the right person, the right skills, and the right cultural fit.

Just think—this could be you. The timing could be right to redesign a job around your skillset to meet the needs of the organization. Win-win!

As you are creating this list, it is important to start thinking about why you would like to work at a particular organization now. Once you have made the list, transfer it to a spreadsheet on your computer that can become a working document that you can share as needed. It will become an important tool for you to track your meetings, conversations, and interviews. From there you can then determine how to reach out and have a meaningful conversation with someone who works for each of the companies on your list. Brainstorm with friends and loved ones and document it all in your notebook and then you can transfer it to your computer for ease of use. Here's how it works. The target company list will be divided in your notebook into three categories/columns, which I call the **Three Ps: Prospects, Pivots, and Passions.** Each organization on your target list will fall into one of these three categories.

The (Usual) Prospects

Under the usual prospects column, you will list any organization or company that feels like a natural fit for you. This could include a competitor in the same industry, a related space, or even a company where you have worked in the past. This is the easiest and most logical place to start your target list because it is likely the most obvious and familiar. For example, if you work for a media and entertainment company, then places like Warner Bros/Discovery, Disney, Viacom, NBC, Hulu, Netflix, and other companies would be a usual prospect. Include any media company that you would like to work for or that feels like a good fit for you. Look at your main competitors in the space and examine whether you would like to work for any of them, and if not, move on to the next.

The Pivots

A pivot is a conscious change in strategy to a different industry, a different role, or a complete change into a new field. It does take a little more thought, introspection, and effort than a prospect, but it's worth it, especially when you're ready for a change.

These are companies or organizations that you may have admired for a while or have a new interest in. Where could you transfer your existing skills into a slightly different industry or organization? This is a great opportunity to research the best companies to work for in your geographical area.

If you're seeking a new job, it means that you're ready for a change for whatever reason, and so it's worth it to explore new possibilities. Again, there are no wrong answers here, so it's okay to dream a bit and consider something a little different or unconventional. While it may take you a little bit outside of your comfort zone, it might just be the perfect stepping stone to your next great career adventure!

Pivots can be intentional, and at other times they may be forced. It could be that your company closes, you get laid off, or a myriad of other situations may have happened. It happened to my husband, Dan. He was working for a well-known media and tech company when we moved to New York, and within five months of starting this job, the company went through major layoffs. He was devastated. We had just moved to New York, bought a new house, and had two young kids and a baby on the way. We were in a tough spot. After weeks of looking for something new and wondering what was going to happen next, we put this strategy to work for Dan. He created a list and began by reaching out to many people in his network and having meaningful conversations about where to go from there. Finally, he received a phone call from a trusted friend and mentor in his network who had been following his career for some time. *Tommy, we are forever grateful for that call. You changed the trajectory of Dan's career and brought him back to Warner Bros. at the perfect time, to take on a new and exciting role working with some of the best in the business. Including you!*

Without doing his due diligence and making the effort to tap into his trusted network, Dan might not have gotten to where he is today. It just takes one person who believes in you to open the floodgates to a better path.

It's not always easy, navigating this career journey and what's next for you, but it is always worth it. As one of my favorite Peloton instructors, Robin Arzon, says, "You have made it through 100 percent of your worst days thus far and you are still here!" (And hopefully are starting to smile a little more as you design your future!)

It doesn't matter if you are a new college grad or a CEO, there's a new job out there for you. Just keep going. Do the exercises in this book, page by page. Put one foot in front of the other, every day. The best is yet to come when you are intentional and focused on where you want to go.

As we discussed in Chapters 2 and 3, one of the major keys to a successful pivot is one of the exercises that you have worked through already. From here, you will want to continue creating a compelling narrative that establishes a clear link between your past, your present, and the reason for your desire to pivot. This story needs to easily pinpoint the connections between your current job and the one you want at the desired company. This compelling narrative helps both you and your prospective employer to better understand the relevance of your skillset and the connection between your current or previous job and the one you want to apply for (or design for yourself!). Since there are tremendous growth opportunities when you pivot, I urge you to carefully and creatively consider which companies to include on this list.

The Passions

This is my favorite part of the Three Ps; exploring your passions!

Under your "passions" column, you will want to include companies that align with your passions or that might enable you to do something that you are truly passionate about. You can keep referring to the work that you have been doing and your Light Log to identify what some of those passions are. Populating this category and helping my clients to explore their passions is truly one of my favorite things to do because they get to embrace one of my favorite concepts, something that the Japanese call *ikigai*.

Ikigai is a Japanese term that blends two words: *iki*, meaning "to live," and *gai*, meaning "reason," which translates to "a reason to live." It's a concept that encourages people to discover what truly matters to them and to live a life filled with purpose and joy. This can translate straight into your career. *Ikigai* combines what you love (your passion, and what lights you up!), what the world needs (your mission), what you are good at (your vocation), and what you can get paid for (your profession), as seen in the following diagram.

In my experience, when we move through the exploration of a client's passions, it is so exciting (for me and for them!) to see their hearts and minds open and light up with the possibilities as they unfold, sometimes with opportunities they never truly thought were possible. I can't wait for you to see what you uncover here as you work through this exercise.

By now you've been exploring this concept of light for quite a while and you understand that what lights you up is like a passion. Understandably, identifying what lights you up or what you are passionate about can be one of the most difficult parts of this process

Source: www.japan.go.jp/kizuna/2022/03/ikigai_japanese_secret_to_a_joyful_life .html

because it requires so much soul-searching. You have been doing this, through the pages of this book. Keep going, it's worth the effort, you've got this!

Remember, if you're still having trouble pinpointing your passions, take a closer look at your notebook, your Light Log, and all the other exercises you have done thus far. What do you see?

- What recurring themes are you uncovering through this process?
- Is there an idea that keeps growing inside of you, that you can no longer ignore?
- What are you most enthusiastic about when you think about your work?

Pay attention to what brings you joy in your everyday life, even the little things. Sometimes when you're stuck, it also helps to get an outside perspective, so I often recommend asking your family and friends for their opinion on questions such as:

- What are my strengths?
- When do I seem most happy?
- What characteristics do my family and friends love most about me?

If necessary, let these thoughts sit with you for a bit—maybe even for a few days—and then go back and check in with yourself again on these themes. From this vantage point, we can take a deeper dive and explore organizations and potential opportunities that you may have never even dreamed of before that align with your passions.

Take your time, let your mind be still, and listen to that inner voice; this is the voice of your heart speaking to you. Sometimes it starts as only a whisper and can be difficult to hear, but give it time; it will become your guiding inner voice and it will get stronger and stronger the more you pay attention to it. It will not steer you wrong.

Let yourself play with the possibilities here. Have a bit of fun with it. The sky's the limit when creating this list. Again, cast a wide net and make the list as big as you want to, and then start to narrow it down as you more fully explore these options. This is an emergent process and takes time, but the benefits will be worthwhile. In addition to helping you design your list; it can also be incredibly interesting to learn about what different organizations on your target lists have to offer.

Once you've identified what companies or organizations to put on your passion list, keep going, and keep adding interesting options for yourself. For each of these categories, and when you have made the list as big as possible, then I recommend that you do a simple gut check. You can do this by closing your eyes and focusing on each passion and each organization on your list and then honestly rating your enthusiasm on a scale of 1–10.

Making Connections

As I mentioned earlier, when making your Three Ps list, this is the place that I would recommend you start using your computer for assistance. Refer to your target list from your notebook and worksheets and transfer them into a working document on your computer. It will be helpful to you in many ways to do this, because it can become a dynamic document that you can share with your family, friends, and growing network and help you keep up to date daily. A shared Google spreadsheet document is my preference, but you can use whatever mode works best for you. This is important because you will want to have a place where you can update and add any pertinent information to your list—for example, links to new articles and news clips, along with company websites and links to your contacts there.

Time to tap into that superhighway of your network!

Once you have completed your target list and classified each company as a prospect, a pivot, or a passion, it's time to begin to look at your trusted network and see who can connect you to people in these specific organizations. Please review Chapter 6 for a refresher on how to effectively utilize your network.

Now that you've done your soul-searching and research on each organization, your goal is to connect with people who work at the organizations that you're targeting. This is up to you to determine how and when you want to reach out, but it can include reaching out through LinkedIn, by email, by phone, or even scheduling a Zoom, coffee, or lunch meeting, as discussed in Chapter 6 on networking.

With each connection and each conversation, your network grows and so does your potential opportunity for a job with each organization. By having these conversations, you will gain valuable insight into what is going on in the industry at large, and what it's like to work at the organization. This data will help you determine if the company you are exploring stays on your target list. This is also why I ask you to cast a wide net (have I said that enough?) and list lots of organizations at first because as you continue you will start to narrow it down based on what you are learning along the way. Then the target list becomes much more real and actionable and then you can start to gain clarity regarding the real opportunities that are out there for you.

While this might seem intimidating at first, it is an essential step in determining which organization is the best fit for you. Also, most people are much more likely to reach out to someone they have previously connected with when a job does open at one of your target organizations—and that could be you!

Many organizations report that referrals are their number-one method of finding great people, and that makes sense in several ways.[1] If you have a great employee who is already successful and happy in your organization, they will most likely be recommending someone else great to work there. Referrals are the absolute best way to find your next job, so working hard to strengthen and develop your network is key. (Apologies to all my recruiter friends out there!)

As a result of this fact, I urge you to take your time and make these meaningful connections when you have an opportunity to do so. Even if you do not ultimately take a job with that organization, this exercise in networking is always beneficial in the long run. Sometimes it really can be about "who you know" and that's okay!

And trust me, at some point in your future, any one of these connections might prove to be even more useful and helpful than you ever imagined. And if it does not end up benefiting you directly, it could potentially help someone else in your close circle or network. Strong relationships are key to business and to life in general, the most important in both our personal lives and our professional lives to have a healthy and thriving life. You cannot and should not take any relationship for granted, because you just never know where it will lead you.

For more exercises and exclusive teachings, visit: MaryOlsonMenzel.com/Resources

Real-Life Examples

What follows are some great examples of my clients using the Three Ps to elevate and recapture their light and move into even more success than they thought possible.

When I started my own business, MVP, in 2012, I took a leap of faith to recapture my own light. I was at a crossroads again. Rather than taking another big global corporate role or working for another executive search firm, with the help of a few friends from Kellogg, I decided to build my own business. *Thank you, Rich S., for giving me the tools and confidence to do this through our work together at Sagin!*

This endeavor was better suited to my current life, dreams, and goals, which considered my changing priorities. When I married my husband, Dan, I suddenly became a mom of two; we had joint custody of two amazing stepkids and shortly thereafter I got pregnant and brought our new baby home, too. I went from zero to three kids in just over a year!

As the kids needed different things at different ages, my entire life shifted. I knew in my heart that with our young kids at home, the big corporate job just wasn't going to work for me anymore. I wanted to be present for all three of them. I had waited until my 40s to become a mom and I wanted to enjoy the moments. We could not necessarily afford for me to quit my job. Besides, I loved what I did, and still wanted to work and to be successful at my job in every way. I wanted to be able to "rock" in the boardroom, but I also wanted to be present at home to "rock" my youngest child to sleep every night. With the prompting and support of Dan, and so many others, I decided to create and design a company—and a new life on my own terms.

My dad, my business mentor and inspiration, had passed away suddenly and tragically in a car accident just before I started the company and I wanted to honor him with my entrepreneurial spirit and make him proud of what I would build. My dad was a huge University of Michigan fan. He went there many years ago for his undergrad degree, and he took us to numerous football games in the Big House when we were younger. In honor of him, my first website was built with the block letters of the M in Michigan and in maize and blue colors.

Making the decision to start my own business felt like I was jumping off a cliff; nevertheless, I jumped, and I have never looked back. It's been a lot of hard work, but also exhilarating and exciting! This was a giant pivot for me, but a necessary step in following my passions to keep my own light shining. To this day, I'm so grateful that I took this leap of faith and followed my own dreams to be both a dedicated mom and a successful businesswoman.

Now we're at the part of the book where you can sit back for a bit, take a breath, and put your feet up for some more inspiration. Here are a few inspiring stories and some snippets of my clients' very real and amazing professional journeys.

Pivoting into More Meaning: Michael

Michael woke up a few months before his 50th birthday and felt a lump in his throat. He was wondering what was next for him. He had a great job at a prestigious magazine in New York City. It was a dream job for many, but on this particular morning, Michael felt something was missing. By all standards, he had it all and he knew it. He asked himself, "What is it that I want for the next ten or more years of my life? What is the legacy that I want to leave with my career?" He was referred to me by a friend from the industry, and the brother of two of my sorority sisters—small world! *(Thank you, Pat H.!)*

Michael hired me and we began a journey of deep decision-making. Should he stay in his current role where he was exceptionally successful, or should he make the tough decision to walk away from a lucrative career to find greater meaning and purpose in his life? We looked at all options and explored all scenarios, and then Michael decided he was ready to pivot to what his soul was calling to him, his greater purpose.

Michael's short-term goal was to be with an organization where he would feel like he could use his many years of experience and expertise to make a difference. We identified his passions and explored the idea of including nonprofit organizations on his list, but we couldn't find what he wanted without having to make a huge monetary sacrifice. Yet one of Michael's long-term goals was to eventually move his family to California, so we kept that in mind as we cast a wide net and explored all opportunities that arose.

Michael was in the process of doing another exercise that I challenge my clients to do, and I would like you to do as well, because it's very important. This challenge is to stay on top of all news regarding the companies on your list, which we discussed in Chapter 4 about your toolbox.

Staying abreast of current news and becoming a student of the industry by researching and following the companies that you are interested in and would like to work for is very important. You can do this on LinkedIn and create a customized newsfeed dedicated to following the companies that you love. You could also set up Google Alerts using keywords to receive updates whenever new information hits the internet containing your keywords. Let me explain how this worked for Michael.

One day, Michael and I were out to lunch with our mutual friend, and Michael said something that gave me the chills. What he said literally stopped me from chewing and gave me a moment of pause. I knew it was something to pay attention to the moment it came out of his mouth. He said that one of his Three Ps "target list" organizations in California had posted an open role on LinkedIn for a publisher of their marquee publication, the *Stanford Social Innovation*

Review. If Michael hadn't been doing the homework by following this organization on LinkedIn and consistently reading their posts, he might not have otherwise learned of this opportunity.

After we talked about it a bit more, I exclaimed, "Michael! This is it! This is the one! This job was made for you!" While he agreed this sounded like the perfect job, he also had a handful of legitimate reasons why it potentially wouldn't work. He said the timing was not ideal and he wasn't quite ready to move to California. That was his long-term plan, but this was now. Aside from that, this job checked all the boxes for him. The timing just felt faster than anticipated.

Finally, Michael ended up applying for the job and was offered the position. He made a bold decision to pivot and courageously moved across the country to pursue a path where his light shines brightly and to fulfill that greater purpose that he was seeking. Bravo, Michael!

It's important to mention that, when I work with a client, I work with the whole person. We don't just focus on their career; we focus on looking into designing and creating a work-life that is tied to all their dreams and needs both professionally and personally. We are all human beings, and our lives don't just stop and start with work. It is all connected and integrated into one life.

A favorite professor of mine from Northwestern's Kellogg School of Business, Harry Kraemer, said, "There is no such thing as work-life balance; it is all about life balance." He discusses balance in the context of understanding all perspectives. That is true life balance, not simply work-life balance, where you are either working or living, but life balance focusing on balancing what is truly important in your life overall.[2] I love this concept and I talk with my clients about it all the time. Your work and your life are intrinsically connected.

Thus, every time I work with someone, I urge them to look at all areas of their life, just like you did earlier in this book. It's imperative. Your career has the potential to fit into checking the boxes of what you need now and what you want for your future in terms of great work, lifestyle, compensation, and fulfillment. You do not have to compartmentalize these areas of your life; they are all an important part of you.

This is where my own intuition, vision, and desire to understand and gain deep knowledge of my clients' lives came in very handy.

We worked through all the options together. Michael and I talked about the pros and cons of the job, the role, the move, and all the other options and factors that would go into making this happen.

Blooming Where She's Planted: Kathy

Many years ago, Kathy heard me speak at a conference for women in leadership. She felt moved and inspired and wanted to meet me, so she reached out and asked for a meeting. Light attracts light, and Kathy wanted to shine brightly. But to have purpose you must do things with intention and look at life from a perspective of what will fill your cup and give you the most meaning.

Kathy told me that she loved what she was doing but just wanted to find a way to move up within her own organization or, if she couldn't move up, to move on to something that she felt she could contribute to in a more meaningful way. She was warm, gracious, and kind and truly wanted to be the best that she could be as a professional. After our meeting, she hired me that same day to be her coach. This put both of us on a trajectory that would change our lives for the better. We jumped in quickly together and began an earnest journey to get Kathy into a place of well-being and greater success professionally.

We explored all of Kathy's options both inside and outside of her current organization. Here are some questions she answered:

- Does it check the boxes in the areas that are important to you from a growth perspective?
- Is this the job that will help create that vision you had for your life?
- Can you find a way to be happier here by finding more meaning?
- Will you find more purpose in the work you will be doing?

Some other questions we worked through were:

- Is there upward mobility where you work?
- Is the culture one that cultivates creativity and excellence in your work?
- Do you enjoy the work?
- Is the commute manageable?
- Is the compensation fair and competitive?

Her answers all came in at a resounding yes. This place checked most of the boxes for her; she just needed a little help navigating her future.

After some soul searching and looking at all the variables in her job and her life together, her answers to the above questions were all confirmation. Therefore, Kathy decided that her best option was to stay where she was and to "bloom where she was planted." So we dug in to work together on how to help her advance and thrive within her own organization. We considered all the organizational nuances and examined all of the players in Kathy's work world. We worked to help her navigate the politics of a large corporate structure and started our regular work together.

When I work with a client, I customize and create coaching programs around their specific needs. Once I got to know Kathy, I saw that what she really needed was an additional sounding board outside of her company to help her navigate the political landscape and create a new, more powerful presence for herself in her organization. We worked to strengthen her confidence and I encouraged her to own her unique light. As a busy executive, she was often too caught up in the day-to-day details and was not always aware of how she was showing up at work—how her unique skills and her authentic voice mattered.

Every month, Kathy would bring me a list of her "challenges and wins." We would celebrate her wins and then we would discuss the best way for her to handle each challenging situation.

At the beginning of this book, you were exploring all of this for yourself as well, by defining exactly what you need from your current and/or future job. No matter where you are, no matter what stage of your career or life, the work you are doing in this book will serve you well on your future path to clarity around what you want and need to create a sense of purpose and contentment in your life and your job. Hold onto this book and your worksheets, and refer back to them often, and at each new stage in your career.

Through the years of working with Kathy, I've not only seen her move up within her organization, but have also seen her grow deeply as a human being. Kathy has gone from being a very talented executive who lacked confidence to a self-assured powerhouse. By shining her own light, she has become a mentor to many of those in her department and someone who loves inspiring others. She is now known as a trusted and inspiring leader to all those lucky enough to be on her team!

Another Pivot Straight into Their Passions: Adam and Stacy

Here is another powerful story featuring a couple who followed their dreams together and made a big, bold move. Many years ago, Stacy and I worked together at the Tribune Company. She worked for a group at the newspaper that had a matrix reporting relationship with our corporate team. To this day, our Tribune alumni relationships run deep; even after we both left we stayed connected, became friends, and saw each other from time to time as we had both moved from Chicago to New York. On one stop of Stacy's career journey she ended up working at Google for a stint in New York City, which is where she met Adam. Her story, the adventure that she and (her then boyfriend) Adam embarked on together, is one worth mentioning and celebrating because it is so inspiring.

They had a vision and they made it happen, and I'm so impressed with the courage and drive that it took to make their dream a very real reality.

"A first step, fueled by passion and possibilities, puts one on the path of adventure."

—*Adam Hersly and Stacy Soberalski Hersly*

After meeting, dating, and spending many years in New York City together, they made the move cross-country to pursue a lifelong dream of living and making wine in the heart of California wine country. This meant leaving behind their family, friends, and everything they knew. Their journey led them from Madison Avenue in Manhattan to Main Street in Napa Valley. They knew it was time to stretch their boundaries, push themselves out of their comfort zones, and make this adventure happen.

How did they do it?

Adam had food and wine in his veins since he was a young boy in New York, where he grew up cooking for his family and had dreams of becoming a chef. Yet he was also passionate about the tech world and ended up following in the footsteps of his father and studying engineering at Cornell. After college, he joined Google, a dream come true for many, but he also knew that his passion for food, wine, and cooking was still there, calling to him from the deep places in his heart.

One day he and Stacy were waitlisted for a wine dinner at Joseph Phelps's restaurant, and they got a call that there was an opening for dinner that evening. They jumped at it. As serendipity would have it, they were seated at the end of the table next to a woman named Lori, who happened to be Joe's daughter. The conversation and the wine were flowing, and one thing led to another. That evening was the first time they met Joe Phelps, the founder of Joseph Phelps Vineyard. After that night, they became friends with Joe and his family. One evening, they were sitting on the patio in Napa and Joe said to Adam, "You wanted to be a chef, but you are an engineer. You should make wine. It is the true combination of art and science." He offered to call UC Davis to get Adam into the winemaking program, and shortly thereafter, inspired by Joe, Adam enrolled in the UC Davis Winemaking Extension program.

Adam began to follow his passion full force and took time off from his corporate job to do internships at August West/Sandler with Ed Kurtzman. Then he took another few months off and interned at the cellar of Joseph Phelps Vineyards. All the while he was being cheered on by Stacy, who fully supported him and believed in this dream.

After all the studying and learning, finally, in 2012, it was time to forge ahead on their own path and Hersly Wines was started. That year was big for Adam and Stacy. They got married, took a leap of faith together, and left their home in New York City to move to Napa full time. Upon arrival in California, they adopted their dog, Mae (for whom one of their first wines was named), and that fall had their very first harvest. They did it! They were on their way to living out the dreams of Adam's childhood.

Adam and Stacy produced an amazing Pinot Noir, the Mae Rose, a great Cabernet Sauvignon, and now a wonderful Merlot. While their dreams were in motion, it was not all simple. An earthquake hit the Napa area, then a global pandemic, wildfires, and a breast cancer diagnosis for Stacy. Through all of this, Adam and Stacy persevered and became even more entrenched in the community in Napa by helping their neighbors and continuing to deepen those relationships as they all went through these times together. They worked hard to make sure they could grow and thrive as winemakers, but also as responsible people, helping their fellow human beings along the way, working through all the obstacles to keep their dream alive.

Charity and giving back has always been an integral part of Stacy's background, and while the majority of Stacy's career has been spent as a global senior leader in human resources and now owning her own HR firm, working to make the world a better place is never out of her focus. Both Adam and Stacy are avid volunteers with St. Jude Children's Research Hospital and so many other organizations in the area. They know how lucky they are to have been able to follow this dream and they give back in every way that they can by asking themselves, "how can I help?".

As they continued to grow and navigate all that came their way, the goal for Adam and Stacy was to bring the wine home to New York, where so many of their friends and family are still living. And they finally made it happen! Their wines have been featured at several prestigious venues such as 11 Madison Park, MASA, the Nomad, the Beatrice Inn, Union Square Cafe, and Del Frisco's, to name a few. They worked hard to create a vision and to make their dreams a reality and now they're riding high, working hard, and having so much fun!

Adam said in a recent interview, "We felt like we finally *made it*! It has been a rollercoaster of emotions, but I am happy we decided to follow the dream and continue to strive forward. It isn't always easy, but it is always worth it!"

Adam goes on to say, "Our style of winemaking is simple. Make what you enjoy and share it with friends and family accompanying good food and lots of joy. We are family owned, and make extremely limited, handcrafted wines. We are some of the new kids on the Napa and Sonoma wine block, but we are making our dreams come true!"

Adam and Stacy say, "We never know what life is going to hand us at any moment, so to us it is important to enjoy it. There is nothing better than having good food and phenomenal wine, and to share both with exceptional people. Family and friends make the world a happy place." In the last ten-plus years, they have been busy bringing their brand to new restaurants and markets around the country, to share their passion with so many. They are proud not only to have been featured in three three-star Michelin restaurants, but also small bistros and "mom and pop" restaurants.

"We are thankful to be able to do what we love with strong passion, living up to the integrity that we promise, and share the fruits of our labor with you! As we say on the back of our bottle, 'Enjoy Hersly Wines in good health!'"

And to this I say, cheers to Adam and Stacy for your inspiring story and for following "what truly lights you up" to make your dreams come true. It's been an honor to watch you both on this journey!

There are so many different ways to make a pivot based on what you want from your life at that particular moment. You get to choose what is best for you!

Marketing to Art Advisor: Brooke

For most of her working life, Brooke was looking for a role where she felt like the work suited her strengths as well as her passions. For many years, she spent too much time listening to her family and friends telling her that she should work in the business world, and that she should go for the money. She was encouraged to take a job with a well-known company.

Brooke was driven toward the arts from a young age. After college, she threw herself into many roles in creative fields. She was an art buyer in the advertising field, a gallery assistant in contemporary art galleries, a photographer's assistant and studio manager for a well-respected architectural photographer, and an account executive at an interactive experiential design firm. Brooke wanted to be around creative people and things of beauty. Even if she was not the creative one, she loved being around people who were.

For a while she held an interesting transitional role combining the experience that she had in marketing with her love of art, working at the Dallas Museum of Art as the marketing director. It was a great experience for her, but it was a steppingstone to what was next for her. At this point, she was still not sure she had found her calling.

The big career pivot came when she moved to New York in 2015. After nearly two years of seeking a marketing role in the art world and not finding anything that felt like the right fit for her, she was discouraged. It was at that point that Brooke was referred to me. With the combined encouragement from her husband, Nick, me, and so many others, she decided to create her own business in the art world. Brooke wanted to bring something new and innovative to the industry. She wanted to offer clients access to great contemporary artists and photographers at relatively accessible price points and to do it in an organic and transparent way. Brooke already had an artist network to start with and wanted to build upon that. She loved the process of discovering new artists and learning about their art practice.

Brooke officially started the business in 2018. Since then, she has worked with hundreds of clients and artists and has sold countless pieces of art. Brooke has built her reputation as an art advisor. Most importantly, she is doing what she truly loves, and not one day of work seems like a chore. Finally, after nearly 30 years, she's found a role that is suited to her strengths and passions. And now, she is expanding, and just hired one of my very best friends, Fiona, to help her build and take the business to the next level!

Everyone's chosen path is different.

This is your story and your life, so you get to do what you want. Sometimes that also means stepping out of the workforce and starting something new on your own. Sometimes that means making less money to have more meaning in your work and life.

More Pivots and Passion Moves

My best friend from high school, Lisa, made a pivot somewhat early in her career. She graduated from college and worked in the corporate world for a few years and realized it was not lighting her up. After she was married and had her boys, she was able to step out of the workforce, write two children's books about kindness to animals called *Love Me Gently: A Kid's Guide for Man's Best Friend* and *Gray Whiskers: A Kid's Guide for Loved Ones Growing Older*. These books uniquely bridge the connection between people and animals. Lisa believes that by caring for a pet, children learn important life lessons of kindness, patience, unconditional love, compassion, and empathy. These lessons help them relate to the people in their lives from childhood to adulthood. Based on the success of the books, she was then able to start a charity called Tails That Teach. This initiative not only gives her great joy, but she is able to make a difference and spread kindness to both children and animals all at once. Lisa's kindness is now a nationwide initiative and she's doing what she loves!

Chris, my best friend from college, has a similar story. Chris had been very successful in the tech and finance world for as long as I could remember. As college roommates, I remember her flying through her finance and accounting classes like a rock star as I was off and running to anchor the news at the university television station. She created a long and lucrative career based on her major and was quite talented and successful. But her true passion was with animals, dogs in particular. So Chris woke up one day in her early fifties and realized it was time for a change. Luckily for her, because of her husband's job and because of smart money management and investments in their savings, money was not an issue, but doing something that she was passionate about and felt meaningful to her was. She decided to quit her big job and dedicate her time to working at a large animal shelter in Chicago. She now works harder physically than she ever has before, but she is shining bright doing what she loves and the animals in the shelter are the happy recipients of her hard work, dedication, and love. She comes home tired, knowing she made a difference, satisfied with her work and her life, and she is sleeping better than she ever has before. She made a pivot that was purely passion based and I'm so proud of her!

We all have our own paths, and our own journeys to take. Each of my clients in the examples above have positively impacted their own lives by taking a realistic look at their lives, being honest about what they wanted for themselves, and then allowing themselves to dream and create a plan to make that dream a reality. They each exhibited great courage and motivation in designing a career that they love, and they were all willing to put in the work to make it happen. They did the exact same exercises and took the same steps I have outlined in this book.

Keep going. Keep dreaming. The next story will be one that you are writing for yourself, and one that will catapult you right into your future. Please share your success story with me—maybe it will even end up in my next book!

As you go on, you will learn more and more about yourself and what you really want out of life by completing the exercises in this book and by reading, rereading, thinking about your work, and checking in with your heart. Does this light me up? Always ask yourself this question first. And always listen to your heart's answer.

I also recommend that you start noticing those around you who seem to have their lights on. Ask them how they got to where they are today. What can you learn from them? I believe that once you open your mind and start paying attention to all the light around you, you will find inspiration in so many places. You may even be surprised by the places in which you do!

Throughout this process you will be challenged, and yes, you will sometimes hit a roadblock or two and want to give up. We are all human. We occasionally have setbacks, but with our lights on, even just a flicker, we can keep moving toward success, day by day. Your life is too precious to waste your time and energy doing something that you don't enjoy. And you are well on your way by now. Let your spirit light the way.

Lights on, YOU!

Summary

These examples illustrate the various directions that Three Ps can take you when you dare to dream. It is truly a powerful exploration and visualization tool to help you find that "sweet spot" at the intersection of what you do and what you love. This target list exercise provides a structure to help you get organized and create a strategic, actionable plan to help you to take the next step in your job search.

Remember the wise words of Lao Tzu: "The journey of a thousand miles begins with a single step." If you are willing to do the work, the process of rediscovering your light and your passion can be such a magical part of your journey. You never know where you will end up, and as the process unfolds, suddenly you'll get clarity, and the path forward will become evident. All you have to do is take that first step and trust in the process.

Discovering, uncovering, and then focusing on your passions can manifest tremendous opportunities that you haven't even considered. The possibilities are endless. I promise, you just have to believe.

9

Shine in the Interview and Land the Job

"Being a star means that you just find your own special place in life, and that you shine where you are."

—Dolly Parton

PART OF WHAT makes my job so much fun is that I get to coach and help people shine on their own unique stage. That stage is not necessarily on Broadway or at Madison Square Garden, but it is a stage nonetheless. Let's keeping moving to help you shine on your own stage!

By this time, you're on a roll! You've explored what you want, are creating a plan, and have started to write the story that is your career history and your life. You've built your target list, have made connections, and are starting to have meaningful conversations. You now know that it's the energy of who you are—your light that will help you to stand out in so many of these conversations.

How are you feeling at this point?

Are you ready to keep moving and take the next step?

Are you feeling confident in the work you've done so far?

How is your narrative flowing as you speak about your story? Is it getting more comfortable for you?

Remember, you are a work in progress and this is a process that is unfolding for you. Your skills, your ability to talk about yourself and go for what you want are building and growing stronger as you go. As you go on, keep working on and fine-tuning a narrative that spotlights your skills and your strengths. Continue to pause, take a breath, and listen to your inner voice, and then keep following what lights you up. Sometimes this process can be uncomfortable and that's okay. *As one of my, other favorite Peloton instructors, Ally Love, said in a recent class that I took, "Don't let your comfort get in the way of your calling."* You are destined to do what makes you happy—it's your calling.

Talking about yourself is not always easy, so it can be challenging to sell yourself in an interview. Sometimes it's hard to let your true light shine because you may be fearful about how you sound, or you don't want to feel like you're bragging. You've been taught to downplay your strengths and be humble. I like to use this quote from Marianne Williamson to help my clients during those times:

> *Our deepest fear is not that we are inadequate. Our deepest fear is that we are powerful beyond measure. It is our light, not our darkness, that most frightens us. We ask ourselves, Who am I to be brilliant, gorgeous, talented, fabulous? Actually, who are you not to be? You are a child of God. Your playing small does not serve the world. There is nothing enlightened about shrinking so that other people won't feel insecure around you.* **We are all meant to shine**, **just as children do.** *We were born to manifest the glory of God that is within us. It's not just in some of us; it's in everyone.* **And as we let our own light shine, we unconsciously give other people permission to do the same.** *As we are liberated from our own fear, our presence automatically liberates others.*[1] [emphasis added]

Let those words sink in. Whether or not you believe in God or a higher power, you are here for a reason, and that is to bring your unique gifts into the world and make it a better place. This is your purpose. Own who you are, in the best of ways, all parts of you, the sunshine and the shadows, too.

As we go into the interview phase, it's important to remember that recruiters and hiring managers are busy, so make the most of the time that you have with them. My days as a recruiter were back-to-back every day and I would work well into the evenings to catch up on everything I needed to do for the next day. Recruiters have to allocate time for meetings with hiring managers, candidate sourcing, screening, interviews, and lots of administrative work to finally get to a successful hire.

Initial phone screens may be only 10–20 minutes and, in that time, if you aren't able to effectively communicate your personal narrative and shine your light in a way that convinces the recruiter you're a potential fit for a role, you likely won't be considered further. This is an important first step, to make it past the first screening. With the first screening, you can also begin to assess whether this company and role are a good fit for you, which is super-important as well!

This is serious stuff. Practice your interviewing skills however you feel most comfortable: with your friends, in front of a mirror, talking to your dog. My husband used to make me do mock interviews with him to prepare and I do this with my clients, too! An authentic, confident, poised, and self-assured persona is what you are going for, always.

Many years ago, I worked with someone who tended to be a bit overly confident. Sometimes he would talk just to fill the space and hear his own voice. Talking so much meant that he ran the risk of losing people's attention. I worked with him on what I call quiet confidence and the power of a sound bite: short sentences or phrases that are easy to remember. When people ramble on for too long without pausing to take a breath, they lose the attention of the interviewer. You want this to be a conversation and a dialogue, not a monologue.

For example, consider the statement "I am known as 'the Mayor' of the office. I know everyone and everyone loves me. I'm the person people go to when they want things to get done. Without me, things couldn't run." It can instead be stated this way: "I am very sociable and am known as the 'go-to' person to help get things done in the office. People know they can rely on me."

There is so much power in the pause. Sometimes, less is more. Taking a breath in between your relevant points is quite. . .(pause). . . powerful. It allows the interviewer to take in and truly digest what you're saying before you move on to the next topic. Let the interviewer lead the conversation and give them enough information with each answer to stay intrigued and to want to ask you more questions.

When in an interview and following the interviewer's lead, answer the question to the best of your ability, and then pause. Don't ramble on or overshare just because you're nervous. We all get nervous at times and that is where the deep breaths and the intentional pause are most important. Deep breaths also help to regulate your nervous system and help you to articulate your thoughts more concisely and clearly. You don't want to seem nervous and/or veer off topic, because you never know where unconscious bias comes in and you don't want to overshare with something that could be detrimental to the whole conversation. Allow them to keep asking the questions and directing the interview. You can only focus on presenting your best self, and telling your story with clear and concise answers; you will most likely leave the interviewer wanting to know more, and you'll likely keep it relevant to the role and the audience.

If your light is bright enough, it can have the potential to wake up even the most stressed-out recruiter and might even just illuminate them in the process, too!

How can you bring your light and energy to the interview to perk them up, you ask? Keep reading, my friend!

When I used to interview people as a recruiter, it was the people who were lit up from the inside that got my attention. If someone had energy and authentic charisma, I would lean in and lean forward and really engage with this person. No matter how tired I was, their energy energized me. I wanted to know more about who they were and what they could bring to the organization.

Let's consider what I call quiet confidence. Some people are born with it; some have to practice it and grow into it. Quiet confidence, humility, and grace come easy to some; my youngest son has this. I might take some credit as his parent, but truly, he's just confident in who he is as a person, regardless of what other people are doing or saying. And for some it's built over the years with experience, practice, and skill. It takes some effort, and some people will do the work and the introspection to bring it into being. When shared and developed, quiet confidence makes your own light feel more authentic and easier for you and for others to embrace. It takes practice, but that quiet confidence in yourself and your abilities is very powerful. And it's with this inner confidence and inner knowing that you can give yourself permission to shine in an authentic way. To spotlight what you are truly good at takes courage and it's also a muscle that with practice you can learn to flex appropriately. You can sell your strengths to a potential employer and still be humble at the same time.

Quiet confidence is a deep inner strength you exude when you speak. It includes being vulnerable as needed, too. It requires admitting what you know and what you don't know and being truthful about who you are and what you bring to the table.

When I meet with someone with that quiet confidence, I'm interested in hearing more. If I get the sense that someone is too cocky or arrogant, it's hard to see past that because I'm not sure if what they're telling me is real. In an interview, it's important to draw your audience in quickly and authentically; otherwise, you'll start to see their eyes glaze over and you will lose them.

Remember, work can be stressful at times and there's a good chance the person in front of you has had a long or stressful day, too, so it's up to you to find the chemistry in the conversation and engage them quickly so they want to spend time with you. Many recruiters are burned out and have a lot on their plates these days. They're overworked, and at the end of the day you're not sure what you're walking into if they've had a long day themselves. You want to be prepared for anything when you walk into someone's office or log into a video meeting. Some hiring managers might not have even read your resume ahead of time and are just winging it because they've been in back-to-back meetings and you might be the eighth or ninth person they've interviewed today. They're checking the boxes, and keep in mind that at this point they might not always be as excited to talk with you as you are to talk with them.

Their time is precious, too, so try to draw them in immediately with who you are and what you can do. This will cause them to want to spend more adequate time getting to know you. People hire people they like. It's the truth. That is our reality. So much of the interview is about connection and cultural fit. Therefore, it's important to make sure you do your homework and know whom you're meeting with to find ways to make a real and lasting connection.

On the flipside, remember that you're interviewing them as much as they're interviewing you. So make a good impression regardless, and be discerning in deciding if this is a person you want to work with. Either way, every interview is a connection and a chance to make a great impression—whether or not you end up working at that organization. This person can become a part of your valuable network, so engage and go for it with gusto.

Consider this: if you don't wow them with your authentic light and shine through the interview, it doesn't matter what your skills are. Think back on Ken—he had the skills, but so did every other executive that we interviewed; it was his energy and his light that put him across the finish line to get an offer.

You are ready for this. Telling your authentic story is exactly what we've been working on.

All roads have led you to this as you have been reading this book—to be able to tell your story clearly and concisely in an interesting and relevant way.

Preparing

What is the best way to prepare for an interview? What kinds of interviews should you be prepared for? What kinds of questions might be asked of you? What kinds of questions should you be asking? The answer to all these questions will vary drastically from company to company, and you need to be prepared for anything.

Interviews come in all shapes and sizes, and you have to be ready to roll with whatever the situation is and whatever direction the conversation takes. I've created a checklist and a guide for you to make sure you're prepared. I'm impressed when someone I'm interviewing has done their homework and I'm kind of annoyed when they haven't, so remember to do your homework and bring your A game to the meeting. You have so much data at your fingertips these days that there are no excuses! You have come this far. Please do your homework beforehand and be as prepared as you can.

Checklist for Interview Readiness

- **Company/Organization:** Do your research; get to know the company you're interested in from every perspective and every angle possible. Make sure you have a strong knowledge of the industry trends for the company you are interviewing with ahead of time.

- **People:** Google and research all of the profiles of the people you will be interviewing with. Check out their LinkedIn profiles and make sure you know who they are, what they've done, and if you have any mutual connections.
- **You:** What are your distinguishing traits and qualifications that will benefit the recruiter, hiring manager, and company if they hire you?
  - o Go back to the list you made earlier and practice selling your strengths. Make the effort to "sell" yourself and tell your story in an authentic way and let your light and passion shine so that people will remember you.
  - o Always use examples from real life. This will add color and credibility to your conversations.
  - o Prepare a list of thoughtful questions to ask them. Use your research to make sure your questions are relevant and appropriate for the interview.
  - o Listen closely to what they have to say, and reconfirm what they say at the end of the conversation. Make sure you understand the next steps and what to do to follow up.

Remember, you don't have to check all the boxes; you just have to let your genuine light shine and make a real connection with the interviewer.

Be prepared for what we call "behavioral-based" interview questions. These are questions that ask you to illustrate a situation using real-life examples that show your true capabilities. Here are some for you to practice responding to:

- Give an example of a goal you reached and tell me how you achieved it.
- Give an example of a goal you didn't meet and how you handled it.
- Describe a stressful situation at work and how you handled it.
- Share an example of how you were able to motivate employees or co-workers in a difficult time.

There are many different scenarios. Select the ones you are most proud of and be prepared to share. Ideally, you should briefly describe the situation, what specific action you took to influence the situation, and the positive result or outcome. Think through these scenarios ahead of time if you can. This is a very popular method of interviewing that has been around for a long time for a reason. It gives interviewers insights into how you have handled real-life scenarios in the past and that is the best way for them to gauge how you will handle things in the future, potentially working at their company.

Remember the sound bites I mentioned earlier in the chapter? This is a good place to come up with sound bites and bullet points for each scenario. I have provided a more in-depth guide to behavioral interviews for you to practice by category.

Emotional Intelligence

EI is the capacity to identify and understand the impact of your feelings regarding thoughts, decisions, behavior, and performance at work in addition to a greater understanding of others, and how to engage, respond, motivate, and connect with them.

- Tell me about a time when you felt confident in your abilities and your work. What was the situation? Why did you feel confident? What was the result?
- Think of a situation you faced where you felt frustrated at work. Why were you frustrated? What impact did you have on the other people who were involved?
- What is an example of something that isn't one of your strengths? What have you done to accommodate this challenge?
- Tell me about a stressful situation you faced. Explain to me how you responded to the situation.
- Tell me about a time when you faced a significant change. What was the nature of the change and how did you react?
- Describe a difficult conversation you faced at work. What was it? What did you do? What was the result?

- How would your current or previous co-workers, supervisor, and staff describe your communication and interpersonal style? Give me an example or two.
- Think of a challenging working relationship you've had. What was your part in the difficulty, and what was their part? Tell me about the person and your interactions with them. What did you do to address the relationship or make it more successful?
- Tell me about a time that your ability to appropriately use empathy turned around a tricky situation.
- Tell me about a time you feel you dealt with an emotionally charged situation. Describe how you were able to transform it into positive emotions and actions.

Flexibility

Flexibility is the concept of being resilient and able to pivot and thrive at a moment's notice if there is a directional change in the organization or on the project.

- Tell me about a time that you had to be open minded and adjust to a new structure, process, or culture.
- Tell me about a time when you had to adapt your style while working with a group of people.
- Tell me about a time you had to change your point of view to consider new information or a change in priorities.
- Give a specific example of how you have helped create an environment where different perspectives are valued, encouraged, and supported. What was the situation? What did you do? What was the outcome?

Creativity

Creativity and innovation go hand in hand. This is the ability to think outside of the box and to bring new and improved solutions to the table.

- Give me a specific example of what you have done to encourage innovation to accomplish the strategic goals and objectives of your organization. What was the situation? What did you do? What was the outcome?
- Describe a time you made a major sacrifice and used creativity to achieve an important goal. What was the sacrifice? Was it worth it?
- Many internal and external factors can impact an organization. Give me a specific example of what you have done when the organization's priorities changed quickly. What was the situation? What did you do? What was the outcome or result? What obstacles and challenges did you face?

Goal Setting and Accomplishments

This encompasses your ability to get things done and to drive results. This is an important skill to help an organization push forward in their achievements and deliverables, thus affecting the bottom line and making a profit.

- Describe a time when you set a goal for yourself and did not achieve it. What happened? Was there anything you could have done differently?
- Give me an example of an important goal you achieved and how you accomplished that goal.
- Describe a time when you set a goal for yourself and did not achieve it. What were the ramifications of your failure to achieve your goal?

- Tell me about a time you were given a goal that you believed would be impossible to attain. How did you handle it?
- Describe how you set your goals and how you measure your accomplishments. Did you achieve your goals? If not, why not? Tell me about a major project you recently finished. Specifically, how did you set the goals and track your progress?

Relationship Management

Trust, understanding, respect, and the ability to build strong relationships and get things done through the power of teamwork is imperative to most organizations.

- How do you go about building relationships with key stakeholders to help get the job done?
- Give me a specific example of a time when it was critical to establish an effective working relationship with others to accomplish the organization's strategic goals and objectives. What was the situation? What did you do? Who was involved? What factors did you consider? What challenges did you face? How did you overcome the challenges? What was the outcome?
- Give an example of a time when you were able to build rapport quickly with someone in your organization.
- Tell me about a time you collaborated with others in different areas or cross-departmentally to determine courses of action to achieve mutual goals.
- Tell me about a time when you successfully gained the trust of a client, key stakeholder, or someone at work.
- Tell me about a time when you were willing to disagree with another person to build a positive outcome.
- Give me an example of how you worked with a difficult direct report or colleague. How did you handle the situation?

Problem-Solving

Every organization will need someone who can take a difficult situation and develop viable solutions to enhance the process and make it work. Problems will arise, it's how you handle them that matters.

- Give me an example of a time when you actively defined several solutions to a single problem. Which solution did you choose and why?
- Give me an example of a time when you used fact-finding skills to solve a problem.
- Tell me about a problem you solved that best demonstrates your analytical abilities.

Project Management

Project management is the ability to organize, lead, and inspire others to get the job done.

- Tell me about a successful program or project that you developed where you had to coordinate and manage a diverse team of people to achieve deliverables.
- What processes are important when implementing a new program across multiple business units?

Keep practicing your answers to these important questions. You want your answers to roll off your tongue naturally and easily.

Even when you think you have prepared for an interview properly and with intention, prepare some more. Some companies love to throw curve balls and see how the candidate handles it. They want to see what you're made of and how you handle the unexpected when you least expect it.

The bottom line is that you have to be able to think on your feet regardless of how prepared you think you might be. Even if you think you're ready for anything, those curve balls can sometimes surprise you.

Years ago, Harvard Business School came out with a 43-page booklet with close to 80 interview questions, including:

- What is your favorite kind of ice cream?
- How would your parents describe you when you were twelve?
- What's the one thing you'll never be as good at as others?

And then more introspective questions, such as:

- How would your friends describe you in three words?
- Describe something that you should start doing, do more of, and do less of.
- Please tell me about three failures you've had and what you learned from them.

Ultimately, you have to be prepared for any crazy question that comes your way, as long as it's legal for the interviewer to ask you. You might be surprised by some of the questions, but you need to be ready to handle them with composure and grace, and to answer to the best of your abilities. Practicing the answers to the questions listed above helps a lot. I'd suggest writing them down and then speaking your answers as well.

At the end of the interview, you still need to have a few questions to ask them if needed. And I'm guessing you're still curious about certain nuances of the job that haven't been covered in the conversation. Here are a few for you to have ready to go in your back pocket if they ask you if you have any questions. Start by asking the interviewer about themself:

- How long have you been with the company?
- What's your favorite thing about working here?
- How would you describe the culture? What kind of personality will thrive in this culture?
- Why is this position open?
- What are your expectations for this position?
- What are the growth and learning opportunities for this position?
- What are the biggest strengths and the biggest challenges that you see in this role, and on this team?

- What is expected in the first 30/60/90 days in this job and by what KPIs (key performance indicators) will I be measured?
- What is the review culture here and how often will I get a formal performance review?
- What is the collaboration style of the team and the organization in general?
- What are the company values and mission?
- What is the company's vision for the future, in one, three, and five years and beyond?
- Is there anything else you need from me at this point?
- What are the next steps in the process?

As you wrap up any conversation, always be appreciative and grateful, and thank them for their time.

No two interviews are the same, but if you're ready and have done your research on the company, the position, *and* the people you'll be meeting, you will most likely do well. Explain to them why you think you'll be a good fit for them in a way that is honest and relevant—and let your light shine from the inside out!

Shining on this stage is not always easy, but with proper preparation and lots of practice, I know you can knock it out of the park. Practice makes perfect!

Even when the interview is done, how you conduct yourself afterwards matters. After the interview, always send a thank-you email within the first 24 hours and, if possible, a handwritten thank-you note within the week. The email is expected, but the handwritten note will give them a second reason to think about you, and adds an element of class, poise, and grace. Handwritten thank-you notes are becoming a lost art. I was always so impressed with those who took the time to add this gesture to the process and I remember them still.

The fact is that we are always on stage. My dear friend and amazing colleague, Victoria Labalme, talks about this in her coaching work teaching people how to Rock The Room® whether your room is with one person or a dozen or hundreds. We are always on stage in every interaction we have, and when it comes to the stage, Victoria is a true expert. Each month she speaks to thousands of people through her keynotes, workshops, and videos. She's got so much wisdom to share, both in her Rock The Room® coaching and in her book, *Risk Forward: Embrace the Unknown and Unlock Your Hidden Genius*. Her ideas are so aligned with the message of this book. Here is one of her insights that is particularly relevant:

Every time you communicate, you have an opportunity to influence people's lives for the better. Long after someone leaves the room or walks away from an interaction with you, your message will live on in their hearts and minds, provided you craft it right. It's time to step into the full extent of who you are and all you can become. The world needs you, not who you think you should be. Don't wait. The insights you're keeping hidden are the ones we want to hear.

When we realize that we are always being evaluated in every meeting we have, whether being interviewed for a job, for friendships, or any relationship, that gives the potential to make a difference in all of our interactions. We should think intentionally about how we want to show up. Show up with your lights on—I know you can!

By now, you're flying along. Hopefully you're feeling more confident about who you are, what you want, and what it is that brings light to your own story and life.

Negotiating the Offer

As you start to get closer to an offer, go back to your notes from the beginning of the book. Use them as your guide, now and into the future, always.

How are you feeling right now? Close your eyes for a moment, take a deep breath, and check in with your heart and your soul. Consider the role for which you have interviewed.

- Can you imagine yourself doing this job?
- Can you imagine working with the people you have met from this company daily?
- Do you feel aligned with the work, the mission, vision, and the values of this company?

- Do you see a future for yourself at this organization? Does this role provide the growth opportunities that you want for yourself?

If this feels right to you, it's time to start to think about what will happen if you receive an offer.

Go back to the list in the beginning of the book:

- Does it check the boxes in the areas that are important to you?
- Is this the job that will help create that vision that you had for your life?
- Will you be happy here?
- Will you find meaning and purpose in the work you will be doing?

If not, can this next move for you be a stepping stone in the right direction? Could it set you up for the next best thing ahead of you? What is the potential for future opportunities and growth?

Not every job is perfect. Not every job will be the be-all and the end-all; sometimes you have to crawl before you walk. I want you to know that every job from here on out is preparing you for the future that you have imagined for yourself—the future that you are creating by reading this book, doing the important work, and learning about yourself along the way.

If this job checks even a few of the boxes and all is going well, you need to be prepared for a potential offer!

This is exciting but can also be tricky.

Let's talk about negotiating the best offer for yourself. I'm referring to the one that gets you excited to turn on your screen and/or go into the office every day. When negotiating with a future employer, it's important to create a scenario that is a win for you within the constraints of the pay scale that they have budgeted for your role.

Here are the things you need to think about:

- The pay, base salary, bonus potential, commissions
- The work itself
- The benefits—health and other
- The upward mobility and opportunity for learning
- The culture
- The joy it might bring doing something with meaning

Think deeply about how this all fits into your life and into the life that you want in the future.

If it's not all perfect for you and you want to negotiate, the easiest places to negotiate are typically not in the base salary but in the intangibles such as more vacation time, continuing training and education (maybe even an MBA), bonus structure, and potential sign-on bonus.

Honesty is always the best policy from the start so you can create a conversation based on trust that will get you to where you want to go from a compensation perspective. You want to be fully transparent upfront about what you are making and what your compensation expectations are, so that there are no surprises in the negotiation process.

Above all, the big picture for what you want out of life is yours, not anyone else's. Many of my clients have been willing to compromise on pay for the opportunity, growth potential, quality of life, and pure happiness potential. Stand firm yet grounded in what you want to achieve in this negotiation.

And sometimes you will decide that your next move looks very different, and you won't be negotiating, but planning your next move to do your own thing, like my friends Lisa and Chris both did (see Chapter 8). Everyone's chosen path is different and it is time to follow your own dream, the one that lights you up. You deserve this!

This is your life. You get to make the decisions that will lead you to your greatest success and the best career adventure for you!

For more exercises and exclusive teachings, visit: MaryOlsonMenzel.com/Resources

Summary

Sometimes it's hard for people to sell themselves in an interview. If that's the case for you, own who you are and remember that your unique gifts will make the world a better place. It's important that you refine your interview skills before getting started. Recruiters and hiring managers are very busy and often have limited time to conduct interviews. It's up to you to spend time practicing so that you can impress them in no time at all. In fact, if your light is bright enough, it can wake up even the most stressed-out recruiter and might even just illuminate them in the process, too.

Prepare for interviews the same way you did when creating your personal narrative. Practice in the mirror or ask friends to do mock interviews with you. The more practice you can get, the better! Study the company or person conducting the interview. Ensure that you know as much as possible about them before you sit down to speak with them. Be prepared to tell your story that you worked so hard to create. Interviews can sometimes have unconventional questions that you can't necessarily be prepared to answer. The behavioral-based interview guide I offer here can help you to prepare for the unexpected.

The power of the pause and quiet confidence go a long way. Perfect the art of these in preparation for your interviews and you will not regret it.

10

Succeed Today

*"You can't just sit there and wait for people to give you that golden dream.
You've got to get out there and make it happen for yourself."*

—Diana Ross

CONGRATULATIONS! YOU'VE GOT the job! Take some time to celebrate!

Your acceptance of a job is the end of one journey and the start of another. Your story doesn't end here, so let's look at what's next for you.

How are you feeling now? Nervous, scared, excited? All of the above?

Have you been to the offices yet, are you working from home, or do you have a hybrid situation? Have you begun immersing yourself into the organization's culture as much as you can, even if it's remote?

Let's prepare for your first three months and beyond by making sure you are successfully onboarded.

Regardless of which path you pursued and where you decided to work, you want to be intentional about optimizing your experience as an employee. The world has taught us that we can think outside the box and create opportunities for employee engagement and connection from almost anywhere. Thus, when you're looking at your situation, you want to think about what scenario works best for you and your organization. Ultimately, only you can decide what might work best for your life, your family, and your career goals. I do know that

101

employers who have "humane leaders" at the helm, will listen to their employees, "meet them where they are," and work to retain their top talent to build a more substantial and robust culture in the long run.

I know it's still early days, but have you started thinking about what you are going to do to keep building your own professional brand, both internally and externally? How are you handling your onboarding? Do they have a good onboarding immersion program? Does the organization have a process to help guide you through your first 30/60/90 days?

Any new job can be daunting, exciting, and sometimes overwhelming, and the first few months are key in navigating the learning curve of any new role. Become a sponge, learn everything you can, and take it all in. In my experience, the first six months of any new job typically had my head spinning for a bit, but paying attention and being open to learning as much as you can and meeting as many new people as you can will help you find your way.

A well-executed onboarding process is key to your happiness and to your retention. In addition to feeling welcomed and connected to the culture, a good onboarding program shortens the path to overall productivity and eventually to upward mobility. Good onboarding procedures help position both you and the organization for long-term success. Decades of data and experience back this up, yet in many organizations onboarding still is often abbreviated or totally overlooked altogether. In a study for Glassdoor by the Brandon Hall Group, researchers found that a strong onboarding process improved new hire retention by 82%. Additionally, it was found that strong onboarding also improved the productivity of new hires by over 70%.[1]

It's important to consult with your new manager or HR leader to make sure you're getting what you need to be successful. And if not, it's up to you to take your onboarding and assimilation into your own hands to be successful.

I feel very strongly about the power of a good onboarding experience. It helps solidify the relationship that was started during the recruiting process, and it helps create a welcoming and important first impression inside of the company itself. In fact, I feel so strongly about the power of onboarding that I helped develop a program for our leaders that we brought into Tribune Company, and it did help quite a bit with retention. And when I started MVP, I made sure that we included onboarding coaching as part of our package for our clients as well!

Organizations spend so much time and money in the recruitment process that it should be imperative that they protect their "investment" in helping their new employees and new executives at all levels feel like they're happy that they said yes to the job. Sonja Gittens Ottley, the head of diversity and inclusion at Asana, said, "Onboarding is a pivotal moment for making employees feel included from day one. It sets the tone for a person's tenure at your company, laying the foundation for their knowledge of and experience working for your company. This is why building an inclusive onboarding experience is so important in creating an inclusive company culture."

Here are some tips to help you find your way in a new company. When my team designs client onboarding playbooks, among other recommendations our suggestions include:

- Work with your new manager to create a schedule for Week 1, including key stakeholder meetings and team orientations already scheduled.
- Clarify any training that will occur.
- Make sure all paperwork is filled out.
- Make sure all technology is ready for you.

It's also so important to find out what you can expect in your first month, including milestones you're expected to hit and any performance review timelines.

- Study the company literature and organizational chart, including bios of everyone you will be meeting and working with, both internally and externally.
- Establish clear goals with your manager and team, along with KPIs (key performance indicators) and put them in writing.
- Ask for regular one-on-one meetings to review company operational details, preferences and goals.

Create a three-month plan that focuses on your top priorities, concrete goals that support your priorities, and measurements for success:

- Make sure that any guidelines and expectations are clarified for your first 30/60/90 days and beyond.
- Use the SMART method with your goals: make them specific, measurable, attainable, realistic, and timebound.
- Keep the lines of communication open with your manager and key clients at every point.

Holding cross-departmental meetings is a big plus because you will find help and people to collaborate with in many different departments if you just open your mind to building relationships. Meet and get to know as many people as possible in your new organization.

When you're meeting people, remember that these are your new co-workers and it's okay to ask them the following questions to gain insight and clarity:

- How long have you been with the company?
- What do you enjoy most about your position?
- What projects are you currently working on that are most exciting to you?
- What are you currently working on that is challenging?
- What excites you most about the future of our organization?
- Do you have any tips for getting up to speed here?
- What do you like to do outside of work?
- What has the relationship between our departments been historically?
- How can we best work together for the greater success of the company and of our departments?
- How can I help you and your department in a way that would make everyone's jobs easier? (Ask this of everyone you meet.)

All the ideas are in an effort to set the stage for your success at your new job. This is the backbone of creating healthy and productive working relationships with your peers from day one.

A first impression is lasting, so prioritize the onboarding experience as you get settled and become your own advocate in your new organization, creating healthy working relationships along the way.

Summary

Keep the positive momentum that you started and onboard with confidence. Be intentional about optimizing your experience as an employee. The first few months of your new job are critical to your success at your new company. If they don't offer a proper onboarding program, then create it for yourself. Consult with your new manager or HR to make sure you're getting what you need to be successful. It's up to you to take your potential for success into your own hands.

Decades of data and experience show that good onboarding procedures help position both you and the organization for long-term success.

If you're responsible for your own onboarding, get meetings on the calendar with your new manager for regular check-ins. Study the org charts and bios of those with whom you will be meeting and working. Clarify training, fill out paperwork, and ensure that your technology is all set up and ready. Beyond that, build out your own 30/60/90-day plan designed to set you up for success in your new role. You've got this!

11

Create Forward Momentum

"Success is not the key to happiness. Happiness is the key to success. If you love what you are doing, you will be successful."

—Albert Schweitzer

FAST FORWARD AND you've made it through the first few months! I hope you've been loving your new job and feel like there could even be more upward direction and wonderful experiences in your future.

What's next? Where do you go from here?

Aside from your 40-hour-plus work week, what else are you doing to develop yourself and keep growing? In this organization you are now working in, how can you spotlight yourself in a way that gets you recognized and promoted, even from behind the scenes or on a screen, virtually, in person, or hybrid? Each situation brings its own challenges and blessings, and it is up to you to decide what scenario works best for you and how you can contribute to the company in the best way possible.

This is an important place to reflect on how you can keep your light on and bloom where you're planted.

Development can be self-driven, company driven, or both. It can be internal or external. These days, in our busy work worlds, you can expect for most of it to be self-driven and that's okay. Leaders are busy and many expect their employees to self-advocate for their own growth and continue to be more productive and engaged, starting from day one and well beyond.

Don't sit back and wait for your manager or your company to make suggestions about learning and growth. Take the initiative and ask your manager what you can do to grow in your role, or to help prepare for the next role. *Remember, our journey does not end when we get the job.* When you want to learn and look for opportunities to grow, it does get noticed by those around you and can also bode well for you in future reviews and next steps in your career. The path of life is a continuous learning journey and at every juncture there's an opportunity for more education and growth. We want to continue to become the best that we can be and embrace that as much as we can!

You're in the Driver's Seat of Your Own Destiny

Many companies these days are doing so much more with so much less. It's a fact that when employees feel like their company is investing in their development and their future, they are more productive and more satisfied in their jobs. And again, if for whatever reason, your employer is not focused on this for you, make the time for your own development. That extra effort will get noticed and could pay off in ways that you never imagined.

There are so many options. If your department doesn't have the budget for executive coaching, look to see what resources there are. Most companies have an internal training group within their human resources or people operations department where you can sign up for onsite or even online training. There are also many options for professional seminars such as the great stuff that our client, Ragan Communications, offers, even two-day training programs, and certification programs that you can attend during the week, at night, or on the weekends.

Don't forget your local or community colleges. There are a lot of adult education classes to choose from and many times if you ask, your company will help with the fees. I teach quite a few of these myself. Reach out to me to find out about how my team can help you! If there is no time or money for coaching or classes, try to learn from those around you. Find a mentor, or offer to shadow a peer or a leader in another department. Take the time to understand what's going on across departments and in other divisions and branches of your own organization. Offer to sit in on meetings and create cross-collaborative opportunities for yourself.

The motivation has to come from within; you can't rely on others to do that for you. And hopefully your company will support your efforts. Once again, even if the company does not have the resources you'd like, take the initiative, and take charge of your own development and your own career. You will not regret it.

Seven Tips to Continue to Support Your Growth

- Keep an open mind. Don't look at your role in the company as only what your position description says. If an opportunity to do more presents itself, jump on it. It could lead to more exposure and an expansion of your skillset, which eventually could lead to a promotion!
- Get involved with others, both in the workplace and work-related clubs. The more people you know outside of your own department, the more this could lead to cross-functional development and collaboration.
- Be proactive in making your leader and the department you work for look good. When you make your manager look good, that only reflects well upon you. As a result, if your manager gets promoted, you could be next in line to lead.
- Help others within the organization. Mentor those who are more junior than you. In addition to helping them further their careers within the organization, it makes you look good. You never know where they will end up and how they may be able to help you at some point in the future.
- Find a mentor.
- Be a team player. Other members of your team will appreciate it and want to help you succeed.
- ABC: Always be connecting.
- Keep your precious network alive, building one inside the organization and staying connected to those outside of your organization as well.

The Three Rs

Here are some additional tips to help you prepare for and negotiate a raise or promotion when you're ready for that next step into the future.

We use the "Three Rs" approach to help our clients move ahead: *review, reach, recreate*.

Review

Are you seizing the opportunities that come with a healthy review culture? If your company has a strong review culture and reward system in place, take advantage of it by having evidence of your accomplishments on hand for those meetings.

If your company has a sparse review culture where managers are less aware of your contributions or even the parameters of your role, take this as an opportunity as well. Request regular meetings and consistent feedback. When you convene, bring your own metrics to share. This will create ongoing benchmarks for your promotion case. Visual examples, case studies, KPIs, and anecdotes will create a conviction that supports your rationale as to why you should be promoted.

Keep a running list of accomplishments and wins throughout the year, including the projects that you have spearheaded, helped manage, or contributed to. Your manager will get a better idea of how you've managed and led virtually (and seamlessly) if you bring context and real data to the negotiation. Even if you work closely with them every day, it's still very important to make them aware of all that you contribute when not on a Zoom call or in their office.

Reach

Are you creating opportunities to raise your visibility with your manager, as well as the entire executive team? Are there special projects you can take on that will amplify and elevate your leadership and skills? At a time when causes are activating so many of us, is there one that is relevant to the business, yet underrepresented at your company?

If so, leading or creating a task force around a meaningful cause can be a tangible and organic way to stand out positively to senior management. Extracurricular projects that benefit the organization and positively engage employees can become the differentiator between similar internal candidates going after the same position.

Recreate

What do you envision yourself doing for the company when you get that big promotion? Bring that vision to life by creating a graphic presentation of what "next" looks like. Describe both practical and boldly ambitious ideas that demonstrate your fresh thinking and unique leadership signature. A presentation is always better than words alone. Be visual, and design a compelling story that will make your manager proud that they chose you to take on a bigger role.

Remember, as a leader you always want to bring solutions to the table. Respect, empathy, and contributions that help your team and your manager shine are proven ways to put yourself on the path to promotion.

Above all, down the road, don't be afraid to ask for a promotion. You are your own advocate in your career, especially while working hybrid or remotely. If you can lay the groundwork ahead of time and create a solid and sensible case for yourself at review time, you're setting yourself up for a more positive outcome and for a potential "Yes!"

If for any reason you do get a "no," use this as a learning experience. Ask questions and find out what you can do to hone the skills or behaviors needed to get a promotion in the next cycle. Make sure you take notes to reflect on, take action, and provide evidence for the next review.

We are currently working with a client who has recently experienced this. He was turned down for a promotion, because, although they loved him, leadership felt that he was just not quite ready to take on this new role. He is using the feedback as an opportunity to build on what can be next for him. And he's now applying to see if the company will sponsor him for his executive MBA to help prepare him for future leadership at his company.

You work hard and deserve to be rewarded for your contributions, achievements, and dedication. Being proactive and bringing solutions and real data to the table will enhance your case for your future and keep your light shining bright.

Summary

Always have a plan and a vision for the future:

- Where do you go from here?
- What are you doing, outside of your job, to develop yourself and keep growing?
- How can you support your work with real data to get recognized and promoted?

This is an important place to reflect on how you can keep your light on and bloom where you're planted.

Development can be inspired by many things. It can be self-driven, company-driven, or a combination of both. Take initiative and ask your manager how you can grow in your role and always keep an eye out for opportunities yourself.

Be your own advocate and look for opportunities for growth in creative ways. Online forums, professional seminars, and adult education programs are widely available options to take charge of your own development.

If a promotion or different role within an organization is the type of development you have your eye on, there are plenty of ways to spotlight yourself at work. Get involved with teams in the workplace and work-related clubs. Be proactive to make your boss and department look good. Find a mentor and look for ways to mentor others when you have the opportunity and help where you can. Remember, your networking doesn't stop when you get the job. Always be connecting!

12

Design a Framework for Success

"The best preparation for tomorrow is doing your best today."
—H. Jackson Brown, Jr.

THIS POINT ON your career journey seems like a perfect moment to share a few exercises that we use when coaching clients to build strength and resilience and set the stage for success as you go for your goals. Setting clear intentions is the foundation for any future planning. So as a first step, as always, I invite you to pause, breathe deeply, and then write out what you want the coming day, month, quarter, and year to look and feel like.

You know how it works by now. You've been doing the work. You understand the importance of continuous learning and creating a vision for your future.

Write out your goals, mission, and vision for your work at your new company or organization. Don't stop to second-guess yourself. Only you will see this list. But by getting it out of your subconscious and onto the page, you will have organically begun the intention-setting process.

You know you're headed in the right direction when you are intentional about your career and your future and make decisions based on truly knowing yourself. As you now know, when you can articulate what you bring to the table and what you want, you can chart the course to where you want to go with greater clarity and conviction.

Life is a journey and when you follow your heart toward what it is that truly lights you up, you cannot go wrong.

Define what success looks like for you, now and into the future of your career. Whether it's hitting specific numbers, wrapping up a big campaign, or completing a major deliverable, it's natural to start thinking about what needs to happen in order to feel like this year (and the many years ahead of you!) are a success.

There's no time like the present to take focused actions that will help you and your team feel positive about finishing strong. Doing so helps you step into tomorrow with even more confidence and enthusiasm.

I recommend identifying two to three achievable objectives that you can back into by creating small goals for each week.

- What do you want to do?
- What do you need to do to achieve this?
- Whom do you need to help you?
- How will you measure and merchandise your success?

Nothing beats putting an actual calendar up on the wall (I like the erasable ones) and making the goals, actions, and accountabilities visible. I guarantee that with focused attention and daily actions, you are bound to deliver results that may even surpass your highest expectations!

Take a Leadership Inventory

I suggest that all executives and team leaders make time for a leadership inventory. It's an intention-setting exercise that reminds you how you want to show up as a leader. Remember, even if you are not leading a team right now, you can still show up as a leader in the organization. Think about what behaviors or patterns are no longer serving you, and what you may want to leave behind in the current year and moving into the next year.

From years of working with other coaches and business leaders, my incredible business partner, Mel Shahbazian, created this exercise to help our clients create what we call the "Leadership DNA" self-assessment to help build a stronger culture of excellence.

It starts with the alignment of the following:

- **What is your north star?** Think of this as your top leadership goal, including who you are and what you want to be remembered for. What is the essence of who you are as a leader and as an organization?
- **What is your mission?** Your mission should be big-picture, long-term, and meaningful. It's your "why."
- **What is your goal?** This is less about values and more about the bottom line. It's actionable and measurable.
- **What is your value proposition?** Prioritize the top values that you hold dearest in your role and for your team. "What lights you up and what special sauce do you bring to the team?"
- **What is your promise?** What is the promise you offer to your employees and to your clients/customers?
- **What is your mantra?** What do you say to yourself and your team every day to ensure that your culture and your leadership are inspiring?

Remember, this is a reflective exercise for you alone. Refer to these exercises regularly, both as a reminder to yourself and to see if anything has shifted or evolved.

Keep yourself accountable, keep growing, and above all keep shining!

Set a Framework for Success

Starting off each position, each project, and each month, quarter, and each year right is so important. Whatever you do for yourself and your teams in the beginning of your tenure at your new organization sets the stage for the rest of the year and your future.

I would like to share another exercise that Mel designed and that she and I use often with clients. This fun and thought-provoking "Mad Libs" exercise gets the creative juices flowing and helps to clarify expectations and set intentions. It's a great individual or team exercise to do during the first few months of your employment, or the first few months of each year at the organization. Plus, it's an enjoyable way to get to know your team and get them all in sync.

"Filling in the blanks" enables a team to identify where their professional goals align with their company's goals. These don't have to line up perfectly, but it is important to recognize the distinction and use that information accordingly. As mentioned, you can do this for yourself and if you have a team, for them too!. If you do have a team, use this as a group exercise, to help get everyone to "buy in" and have alignment right out of the gate.

Individual Goals

- My goal for my work is _____.
- The biggest reason I chose this is _____.
- Previously, the three things I was most proud of was _____.
- I also faced three big challenges in the form of _____.
- Achieving this goal would mean _____ for me. It would mean _____ for my life, and _____ for my business.
- One behavior I must eliminate to achieve this is _____.
- One behavior I must cultivate to help me achieve this is _____.
- My bucket list wish for my work is (dream big here!) _____.

Once you've gotten clarity on your personal goals, look at what you want to achieve in the workplace. If you have a team, how can you be just as intentional about driving results for yourself and your team?

Get very clear on what success looks like so you can create a plan to help you achieve it. Remember, you are not alone. Include your teammates and colleagues in this planning as well. Understand each team member's motivations and strengths and assign them tasks accordingly to help move forward together.

Team/Organizational Goals

- My team's goals for the business are _____.
- The biggest reason we chose this is _____.

- In the past, the three things we were most proud of were _____.
- As a team, we also faced three big challenges in the form of _____.
- Achieving these goals would mean _____ for our team and _____ for our business.
- One behavior we must eliminate in our team/culture to achieve this is _____.
- One behavior we must cultivate in our team/culture to help us achieve this is _____.
- Our bucket list wish for our team is _____ (dream big here!).

Now that you have reflected and put intention into your goals, you can create a strategy for how to make it happen. Try not to get overwhelmed. Break it into baby steps and tackle some every day. This is how we make progress! Set up bimonthly or quarterly meetings to check in on progress and support each other in your shared resolutions.

All you need is an hour, a whiteboard, and an open mind to set a framework for shared success.

We regularly do this exercise with our coaching clients within the context of their current roles. I've also asked my own team at MVP to complete it, and I do it myself every year. In addition to helping create your plan and define your intentions for the remainder of the year, it can also become the foundation for your professional success plan in the coming year.

Here are some additional tips to get you started and help you stay on course:

- Always start with a vision and a plan.
- Review your goals from last year and create a measurement of what success looks like for this year.
- Curve balls will come your way. It's how you handle them that matters.
- Stay flexible and creative.
- Take calculated risks and learn to pivot quickly.

- Become a student of your industry and learn from your competitors, too.
- Focus on great customer service and operational excellence by getting to know your client or audience in a meaningful way.
- Stay organized and take notes to reflect on for continuous improvement.

Consistent check-ins and an openness to recalibrating and rerouting as needed will help keep the process fluid and moving ahead in the right direction. With clear intention, deliberate planning, and the right people in place, you can set yourself up to achieve your goals and more.

Here's to setting your intentions, clarifying what success looks and feels like, staying on track, and keeping yourself accountable. These leadership behaviors will deliver dividends to you and your teams throughout the year and right into the next year.

To your continued success! Keep it going!

**For more exercises and exclusive teachings, visit:
MaryOlsonMenzel.com/Resources**

Summary

Now it's time for you to focus on the success you create and your future planning where you are right now. Write out your goals for your work at your new company. There are no wrong answers; don't second-guess yourself. This is for your eyes only. You have done the hard work and know you are headed in the right direction, so be intentional about what happens next. I encourage you to take a leadership inventory by designing your "leadership signature." In this exercise, you'll align your north star, mission, goal, value proposition, promise, and mantra to set up a framework for success. You can also complete our MVP-SPARK "Mad Libs" exercise to get your creative juices flowing. These exercises will surely help to build your strategy and future planning. They can even help your team to do the same.

Cheers to your success!

13

Give Yourself Grace

"Keep your face always toward the sunshine—and the shadows will fall behind you."

—Walt Whitman

YOU ARE CONTINUING along on your journey, at a pace that works for you, but what happens if you hit a speed bump? What if you begin start to feel stuck at any point in this process? Or even stuck in your new job that you thought was the dream job? There may be times that you feel stuck. This can happen to all of us. Many of us have been there at least once if not multiple times in our careers and our lives. It might be happening to you at this moment, but you are now armed with the tools to help yourself out of any situation and reassess where you want to go from here.

No job is perfect, so rather than letting yourself feel down or getting too focused on what's not working, let's think about how you can keep moving forward, learning, and growing from your experiences. There is not just one direction; you get to choose where you go from here. There are always other options out there for you to explore.

The Side Hustle

Perhaps you took what you thought was the role of your dreams, but it turned out to be less than you expected. Maybe you've recently discovered that there's something else that lights you up even brighter than this current job. Sometimes the job that you need to keep the lights on in your house doesn't quite light you up inside, but pivoting big may not be an option at the moment. If that's you, then this is the time to look for other ways to keep your light on. This is when a side hustle becomes so important.

These days, lots of people have a side hustle to help them earn extra income, do something else that they love, develop new skills, dip their toes into something outside of their "day job," and then eventually or potentially quit that job to move into something more fulfilling. Remember, you are always setting the stage for your future success.

A side hustle can be something that you are passionate about, and it can also help to lead you to what is next.

The side hustle is becoming more and more acceptable in our gig economy and at times it becomes imperative to make enough money to stay afloat. Sometimes it's just an outlet for you to continue to pursue your passions in a way that gives you energy. A side hustle can be an alternative job to help you live your passions and make some extra money, or it can be used as a step along the way on your career path journey. Sometimes it can be a way to dip your toe into something new before you make that giant leap. And sometimes it's exactly what you need to prepare yourself for your future and what's next. It takes the pressure off having the perfect job right now and gives you the purpose to start working on a plan for what could be next for you, something that might be even better than where you have landed today. Remember, this is a journey—your journey—and I'll keep reminding you that you get to choose which direction to take next.

Pivoting

My friend Michael Clinton wrote a great book called *Roar into the Second Half of Your Life (Before It's Too Late)*. In this book, he discusses creating an actionable plan to make the second half or any future part of your life happy, fulfilling, and productive. This book to me is about planning and preparing for whatever you want next, and I think that his advice is good for anyone who wants to make a long-term plan to pivot out of their existing work—whether or not you're ready for retirement.

It's never too late to dream a new dream or pivot, reinvent yourself, and find a rewarding new career again and again. Many of the skills you've acquired in previous positions could be transferable, but don't worry if there are gaps in your knowledge. You can also think about going back to school to obtain a qualification in a field that interests you. No matter your age. This is your life and your plan, and you get to design your own path with all of its beautiful twists and turns and ups and downs.

Your light may dim at times, too, sometimes to just a flicker. But don't be afraid; understand that this might be a stage of life or a moment in time to give yourself grace and be patient with yourself. Give yourself the same kind of grace that you would give to others you love and go easy on yourself as you move through the experience of whatever is happening in your life. You are now well versed in figuring out how to identify what lights you up, so if there is a situation that gives you pause, you will start to know better how to identify it, to pivot into the next adventure, and to shine bright again.

Remember, even when you are truly lit up, life can surprise you with unexpected and unplanned circumstances. Inevitably, there will be challenges in the future. But now you know the signs and what to do if this happens to you. After all of the work you have done, you will feel it when your light starts to dim, and you will course-correct more easily. You will know how to adjust your sails and make sure that you can pivot much more quickly than you did in the past, or maybe even sail off into the sunset into a second or third act that you never even imagined before.

And now I'm going to move you to another vision, from a sailboat to a racehorse. Stay with me here.

Remember that you are born to run. You've been moving through your life and into your career like a beautiful and majestic racehorse who has won its share of championship races. It can be a wonderful time in your life where you get to take off your blinders in a wide-open meadow, take a little break, and pick your head up to look at the scenery surrounding you and help broaden your perspective on work and life.

The Importance of Self-Care

When you begin to feel out of balance or a little off course, go through the pages of this book and your notes and do a real "gut-check" to help you course correct and find your way down a potentially new path.

And just remember that, occasionally, life throws you a few curve balls—sometimes several all at once. It happens to all of us.

In the summer of 2023, this happened to me. While I was so grateful for a very busy schedule, lots of work, a thriving coaching business, and the usual happy chaos of family life, it was a torn ACL and meniscus, the tragic and sudden death of my beautiful niece Stephanie, coupled with the added stress of my aging mother being hospitalized multiple times in Chicago that forced me to call a time-out for myself to take a breath and regain my own strength and resilience and do a little of my own recalibration.

It's times like these that remind you of what is truly important in life. And when the curve balls come, it's how you handle them and what you learn from the tragedy or the trauma that matters.

Therefore, as I get older, I believe that balancing out the busy seasons of work with some planned downtime is very important to maintain not only my physical and mental health, but also clarity about my career and my personal life.

When I took that time off, I spent my days with my family relaxing, recharging, and reconnecting on Block Island, a magical place in Rhode Island that we love. Doing so enabled me to come back with my light switched on and refocused on how I can bring that light not only to my family and friends, but also to my clients, and my work, doing what I love.

- How are you staying connected and motivated during the tough times?
- How are you creating balance for yourself to find resilience when you need it?
- What are you doing to refresh your body, mind, and spirit so that you can bring that balance back to your life, your teams, and your workforce?

Some of my favorite ways to practice self-care are quite simple and you can do them from almost anywhere. The important thing is to create an intention and follow through with this commitment to yourself and your well-being, for your sake and the sake of all of the people around you.

Morning meditation: What better way to start your day than with an inspiring and motivating meditation? Daily meditation has been proven to offer so many benefits to your body and mind. It not only reduces stress and anxiety, but research shows that it also helps enhance your mood, promotes healthy sleep patterns, and boosts cognitive skills. I personally like the Insight Timer app. It has thousands of guided meditations from great teachers and will help you apply your renewed clarity to daily life.

Move your body: Immediately after my meditation, I pop out of bed for a workout before I start my workday. I feel more balanced, uplifted, and energized all day. In addition, morning exercise means that I'm getting my workout in and not being distracted by work or family as I might be later in the day. My workouts consist of riding the Peloton, weight training (a must, especially for women over 40!), yoga, Pilates, or a brisk walk with my dog.

Massage it out: For those of us with busy schedules and lives, a regular massage, if you can swing it and afford it, is also a really great way to practice self-care. If massage is too rich for your budget, Amazon has a few great products that you can buy for under $100 dollars to do it yourself at home. (Sometimes I even pay my son for a quick shoulder rub when I am feeling extremely tense!)

Connect with loved ones: And finally, spend time with family and friends. Surrounding yourself with people who love, appreciate, and want only the best for you is a fundamental way to unplug and recharge. Laugh and unwind a bit after a long work week. Research shows that having a strong social network can help improve your mood and provide a sense of belonging.

How does this translate to the workplace and to your work in particular? Nurturing yourself at work and at home—and with your team if you have one—by practicing reflection and gratitude will inspire them and contribute to better results and greater overall success.

Humane Leadership

These powerful tools of self care and introspection are the hallmarks of empathetic leadership and what Mel, our colleagues and I like to call "humane leadership."

To us, a humane leader exemplifies the following traits:

- Empathy
- Humility
- Compassion
- Emotional intelligence
- Authenticity
- Vulnerability
- Openness
- Approachability
- Integrity
- Supportive
- Deep caring
- Transparency
- Respect
- Resilience
- Relatability
- Kindness

Humane leaders ask: What does my company really stand for, what do my people stand for, and what do I stand for? Humane leaders are values- and mission-driven leaders who get the best out of their people by being vulnerable and flawed and allowing that same "humanness" to be expressed by their people.

As a good leader and a truly humane leader, you can motivate and inspire others and embrace and appreciate the gifts in every situation. Truly listen to your co-workers with the intent to get the best outcome. With authenticity and vulnerability, humane leaders know that our journey isn't always linear and they embrace opportunities for growth everywhere they see them. They proactively practice resilience while riding the waves of both personal and business ups and downs. And as a leader, it all starts with you.

If you can do so, every once in a while, take a little time to reassess or continue to fine-tune what's important in your life, both in the workplace and at home. It doesn't have to be a hiatus; it can be a weekend, a day, or even a few hours. Encourage your team members to do the same. A little self-care, and time away from the office to reflect, will pay off dividends with productivity and results when you do come back to work.

Focus on Gratitude and Goals

Consider organizing a Gratitude and Goals meeting, where every team member has the opportunity to look their colleagues in the eyes, tell them what they appreciate about them, and give examples about how they've had a positive impact on their work this year. After they've gone around the room expressing gratitude, it's time to brainstorm one thing that each team member can do to help achieve team goals and create success for the rest of the year:

- What's your focus now?
- Where are you headed at this point?
- How can we help each other get there?
- Where do you want to be this time next year?

Those big plans, goals, and benchmarks you started planning for in the last chapter will benefit from your review of what's been working, and where improvements can be made. Tweak what you can now so you end each year on a high note!

What's important is that when life throws you those curve balls, you find a way to keep your light shining and come back full speed ahead, having learned and grown from whatever it was that happened.

You can achieve your goals, but you can also be kind to yourself, and assess where you are today, personally and professionally—the challenges, the opportunities, the progress, and the silver linings, too! Doing so will provide the perspective you need to design your future in a way that works for you and your unique leadership style. The future will be here before you know it, and being prepared and intentional about what you are doing, how you are feeling, and where you are going will help you achieve the best results.

Ask yourself, "What does your light signify for you now and how brightly is it shining at this moment?" After you've answered the question, take a deep breath, pause, pat yourself on the back, and give yourself credit for reigniting, again and again.

Summary

If at any time, you start to feel stuck in this process, stay calm and begin to create another plan. We all get stuck sometimes. You have the tools you need to start over in this process, if necessary. And there are plenty of things you can do for support as you navigate this time.

Keep your light on with a side hustle. Let's say you took what you thought was the job of your dreams, but it turned out it wasn't. Or perhaps since taking the job, you've discovered something that lights you up even brighter. Pivoting big may not be an option at the moment. Sometimes the job you need to keep the lights on in your house doesn't quite light you up inside. If that's you, this is the time to look for other ways to keep your light on. This is when a side hustle becomes so important.

A side hustle can be an alternative job to help you live your passions and make some extra money, or it can be used as a step along the way on your career path journey. Sometimes it can be a way to dip your toe into something new before you make that giant leap. And sometimes it's exactly what you need to set the stage for your future and what's next. It takes the pressure off having the perfect job right now and gives you the purpose to start working on a plan for what could be next for you.

Nurturing yourself at work and at home by practicing reflection and gratitude inspires you and your team to contribute to better results and greater overall success.

You are doing great!

14

Practice Gratitude

"Gratitude makes sense of our past, brings peace for today, and creates a vision for tomorrow."

—Melody Beattie

GRATITUDE IS A choice. We have the power to choose how we feel and how we react to everything around us on a daily basis. A dear friend said to me recently, "You cannot have faith only when things are going your way. You must also have faith even when they are not. Optimism and gratitude are inextricably linked and are generated from inside of you, not from outside." Wise words, Chris, and I'm so grateful for our lifelong friendship, ever since our days working at Software Architects together.

Gratitude is also "the practice of making space for appreciation," according to psychologist Dr. Snehal Kumar. This could be an appreciation for the people and things in your life, the experiences you've had, or the experiences you've yet to have, but gratitude can also (and should) be rooted in an appreciation of the self, Kumar explains.

With every situation, even the most stressful, I try to believe there can be a silver lining or some sort of lesson to be learned that will lead us to where we need to go to be the best that we can be. It may not be immediately clear when we are going through it, but eventually, hopefully, it will all make sense. I don't want to sound cliché, but there is something to learn in every situation that comes our way. It's not always easy to see it when we're in the middle of it, but after reflection, there can be moments of understanding, acknowledgment, and even some peace because of what you've been through and how you got to the other side—even when you felt like you couldn't.

I had a recent situation where I was asked to be a part of a prestigious board. I wanted to say yes, but something was nagging at me that it would be too much. I had work, kids, family, an aging parent, and a book deal on the way. I had to take the advice that I give to my clients and really listen to my heart and follow my intuition. As much as I wanted to say yes, I knew I had to say no to be available and present for the other parts of my life that demanded my attention. The day after I said no to this opportunity, for all the right reasons, another opportunity fell into my lap that would demand less attention, but also one that made me light up even more!

Sometimes the Universe gives us tough decisions to clear the path for something even better.

Michael J. Fox, who has been through his own health battles, said, "If you don't think you have anything to be grateful for, keep looking. Because you don't just receive optimism. You can't wait for things to be great and then be grateful for that. You've got to behave in a way that promotes that."

Light attracts light. Being grateful for both the small things and the big things creates more to be grateful for.

My life has not always been perfect; it's a work in progress, but through a divorce, several moves across the country, job changes, battling and surviving breast cancer, several car accidents, the tragic death of my father, the loss of a sibling and then my niece, and now the very raw pain of losing my beautiful mom as I edit this book, I am still standing—and you are too regardless of what you have been through up to this point. None of it has been easy, but I know that I want to learn to accept and grow from every experience I have, even the hard times. I want you to be able to embrace this notion, too. I try to focus on moving from grief to gratitude. Always.

And after whatever you have been through, you are still standing and looking to make your life better through the pages of this book, too. That is something to celebrate. Every. Single. Day.

There is a lot of research out there that tells us that practicing gratitude can have a profound impact on our overall well-being.

People who regularly express gratitude report feeling happier, more optimistic, and more satisfied with their lives. They also tend to have better relationships, sleep better, and experience fewer symptoms of stress and anxiety.

Here, I'd like you to pause. Embrace where you are at this very moment and find at least one reason to be grateful. Write it down now, in your notebook. Keep finding reasons to be grateful in your life, no matter how big or small. They are worth celebrating and appreciating.

Life will surprise you at times. It's up to you to decide how you will handle it and where you will go from here. As my colleague, Mel and I often say, "When life gives you lemons, it's up to you to figure out how to make the lemonade." (And then, if you want, add some vodka!) Once you have done so, drink it up, savor, and enjoy every last drop. Savor the beautiful moments in your life every day, even if they are small.

I heard something recently with my son at church, and he repeated it back to me in a moment that I had been struggling with what to do about my mom and how to help her through this final stage in her life with grace and love. "A pessimist sees a glass of water as half empty, an optimist sees the same glass of water as half full, but an optimistic 'opportunist' sees the cool refreshing water filling the cup and decides to drink it and enjoy every drop and then shares that abundance with others." With that reminder, I packed my bags and flew to Chicago to see my mom, thanks to the wise prompting from Christopher to take advantage of the time I still had left with her. No regrets. You do the best you can in this precious life, and I am grateful for every day with the people I love and for a son who seems to understand more about life than some adults I know.

It's not just about the big things and your accomplishments; it's also about being grateful for the little things and creating intention around how you react to the unexpected. Allow yourself to slow down long enough to take it all in. Enjoy the rainbow, and every little bit of sunshine after the storms of life have passed.

My son laughs at me because I am constantly noticing the beauty all around me, from the color of the changing leaves to the sparkles of the sunshine coming off the water. A deep exhale and a good cup of coffee. No matter what it is, find the beauty and enjoy the moments daily.

Marshall Goldsmith, coach, leadership guru, and founder of the MG 100 Coaches group that I am a member of, said, "Gratitude is not a limited resource, nor is it costly. It is as abundant as air. We breathe it in but sometimes we forget to exhale." Let's not forget to exhale.

Take a deep breath and start to pay more attention to the beauty all around you. Once you start to notice the simple beauty in the moments, your life will transform, and you will start to see beauty and goodness in places you might never have imagined.

This doesn't just happen in nature or at home; it happens at work, too—the smiles of your co-workers, the satisfaction of a job well done, the praise from your manager. Embrace and enjoy it all, both the little things and the big things. It is all of the little moments in between that make up a joyful life.

In their book *Leading with Gratitude: Eight Leadership Practices for Extraordinary Business Results*, my friend and colleague from the 100 Coaches, Chester Elton, and his colleague, Adrian Gostick, talk about how to bring gratitude to everything you do. They say that practicing gratitude is a simple way to reinvigorate our professional, personal, and social lives. They also mention that Robert Emmons, a professor at the University of California Davis, points to the results of several studies of more than two thousand people to show the value of keeping a gratitude journal (or a "Light Log"!). Emmons says that the benefits from counting blessings are tangible, both emotionally and physically, and that people are 25% happier and more energetic if they keep gratitude journals, have 20% less envy and resentment, sleep 10% longer each night and wake up 15% more refreshed, exercise 33% more, and show a 10% drop in blood pressure compared to those who are not keeping these journals. Thus, Chester and Adrian have also recently come out with a workbook for this called *The Gratitude Habit: A 90-Day Journal to a More Grateful Life*. In it they say, "Gratitude is the compass that directs our hearts toward the abundance that surrounds us, reminding us to cherish every moment and find joy in the simplest of gifts."

Emily Fletcher, the founder of Ziva, a meditation training site, mentioned in one of her publications that gratitude acts as a "natural antidepressant." The effects of gratitude, when practiced daily, can be almost the same as medication. It produces a feeling of long-lasting happiness and contentment, the physiological basis of which lies at the neurotransmitter level.

When we express gratitude and receive the same, our brain releases dopamine and serotonin, the two crucial neurotransmitters responsible for our emotions, and they make us feel good. They enhance our mood immediately, making us feel happy from the inside. By consciously practicing gratitude every day, we can help these neural pathways to strengthen themselves and ultimately create a permanent grateful and positive nature within ourselves.[1]

Mel has another exercise, called the ABCs, that we like to do to help promote gratitude at work. It's something I hope you'll start to do on a regular basis:

- **Achievements:** What have you done this year that hit or exceeded your goals? What are you most proud of?
- **Blessings:** What are the things, people, or situations in your life and workplace that you are grateful for? The moments of human "being" and not "doing."
- **Commitments:** What will you commit to that will get you to success for the year? This is something that you can always come back to, for yourself, your family, and your team. Simple exercises to keep you motivated and on course at any stage of your career journey.

Try it for yourself, with your family and with your co-workers and teams. You'll be happily surprised at where you can find the blessings in your life.

My dear friend and colleague, Dr. Mark Goulston, who passed away while I was writing this book, designed something called a **Power Thank You** that he taught me and together we took quite a few executives through this exercise. It is truly quite "powerful." Essentially, Mark says in his book *Just Listen: Discover the Secret to Getting Through to Absolutely Anyone* that when you do this, your words will generate strong feelings of gratitude, respect, and affinity in the other person by following these three simple steps:

- **Part 1:** Thank the person for something specific that they did for you.
- **Part 2:** Acknowledge the effort that it took for that person to help you by saying something like, "I know you went out of your way to . . ."

- **Part 3:** Tell the person the difference that their actions personally made to you.

Mark was very appreciative of our friendship, our work together, and of life. He challenged us all to do this on a regular basis. He said to begin by thinking of the person who has helped you the most over the last month, and then the person who has helped you the most over the past year, and then the person who has helped you most over your lifetime. He suggested that we can start there and offer each one a "Power Thank You" in person, by phone, text, mail, or email.

Why not get started now? You can read more about this in his book *Just Listen*.

I offer a power thank-you to you for reading this book, and for doing the work to create a life that you love!

Summary

Gratitude is a choice. It may not be immediately clear, but in hindsight, there will be moments of understanding and acknowledgment.

Take time to pause and embrace where you are at this moment. Find a reason to be grateful and memorialize it in your notebook. Don't stop finding reasons for gratitude. Sometimes the Universe gives us tough decisions to clear the path for something even better.

It's both the little, less obvious things as well as the big things like your accomplishments that matter. Take a deep breath and start to pay attention to the beauty around you at home and at work. Once you start to notice the simple beauty in the moments, your life will transform. You'll start to see goodness in places you might never have imagined.

Embrace the goodness in the moments and appreciate that you are building the life of your dreams—right here, right now!

Conclusion: Lights on for Life

"As we express our gratitude, we must never forget that the highest appreciation is not to utter words, but to live by them."

—John F. Kennedy

Wow. You DID it!

Here we are, at the end of the book, and the end of our time together for now. Congratulate yourself for all your hard work; you're making it happen, day by day. I'm so happy for you, and so grateful to have been on this journey with you through the pages of this book. I know it wasn't all easy, but you put in the work, and you made the effort to reflect and design a brighter future for yourself, and are now starting to bring it into existence. Even if you're not quite there yet, you're on your way, and that's what matters. Each step of your journey should be applauded and celebrated. I am applauding and celebrating you right now.

Hopefully, now, you have the job of your dreams—or at least a job that lights you up and is the stepping stone moving you in the right direction to your next great career adventure. Every step of the way, keep paying attention to what gives you joy, to what fills your cup and gets your head off the pillow each morning.

Pay attention to your light. What is happening to your spark? Is it shining bright, just flickering, or starting to dim? Let your light be your guide to what is working for you in your life and in your daily work.

How are you feeling about your work? Are you enjoying it? What can you do to keep that light on? What can you do to continue to bring joy and purpose to your days on a regular basis?

Take a long deep breath, exhale, and relax deeply into a job well done.

And then keep going. This is your life and you are on a journey that can keep getting better for you with intention and an ongoing strategy.

Keep a vision for your future and keep striving for the life that you want. Keep dreaming—what comes next for you is in your hands, and remember Zig Ziglar's words: "If you can dream it, you can achieve it."

Keep that mantra and any others that speak to your soul in your head as much as possible.

Ask yourself the following questions that Marshall Goldsmith—leadership guru, coach, and the founder of the MG 100 Coaches—asks himself every day. Did I do my best to:

- Set clear goals?
- Make progress toward goal achievement?
- Be happy?
- Find meaning?
- Build positive relationships?
- Be fully engaged?

Keep striving to be the best you can be. Keep learning and staying curious. Enjoy and celebrate the moments—the big, the little, and even the mundane. They're all gifts if you choose to look at it that way. Stay present in the moment and in your work. Create more and more joy by paying attention to the work you are doing and keep doing it with passion and enthusiasm. This is your life, and you get to enjoy it to the fullest. As you should.

Look for ways to help others on their path, find purpose in the day-to-day, and make work fun. Bring your own style into the workplace and shine your light for all to see and experience the goodness that you bring, just by being yourself.

As is mentioned many times in this book, when you find joy in your work, people notice. You have a much higher potential to be recognized for it and you will inspire others to do their best as well. I have seen this over and over again in my work with my clients, and in my family.

I see it in my husband, Dan, living his best life at work and enjoying his boat; my now-14-year-old son, Christopher, as he finds deep joy in his life, surfing and playing lacrosse, giving his all to everything he does and with a smile on his face; my 22-year-old stepson, Connor, who just knocked his internship out of the park and graduated from college; my 24-year-old stepdaughter, Sam, who just got into the school of her dreams for her master's degree in social work; and my 98-year-old mother, Veronica, who passed away while I was editing this book, who had the sparkle in her eyes and was still slowly doing her artwork up until the very end. You all and so many others are my inspiration.

And now that you are on the path to staying "lit up," it's your turn to pay it forward.

As I've mentioned, when you look for opportunities to strive for greatness and purpose, you unconsciously help others get there, too. You make the world a better place by doing what you love. This is how it works. But let's take it another step further. Let's look for ways to help others. Let's look for ways to pay it forward to those who could use some help. It's time—time to spread that light to others, one smile at a time, one day at a time. When you're shining, people will continue to notice you more; people will be inspired by you. You are that person who walks into a room and lights it up. Shine that brilliant light of yours onto everyone you meet, and it will come back to you. One person at a time, you can help brighten this world.

When we're lucky enough to be given much, much should be given back. I often think about the quote from the Spider-Man movies: "With great power comes great responsibility." When we're lucky enough to be able to follow our dreams and do what we want, we must look to help others do the same.

My wonderful client Libby always quotes her dad saying, "When you reach the top, you have an opportunity to reach back and grab the hands of others to lift them, too." He told her, "You always have a choice to help others and make it different or easier for someone else." What a beautiful sentiment that helps make the world a better place.

I know that Libby lives her life with her father's words every day at the office and at home. And you can, too! People come along at different times and stages of your life who will continue to show up and help you navigate through to the next level of your career. Don't ever forget those people. They are the unexpected helpers and guides who come with their flashlights on to help light our way.

Look for people who will guide you from here on out. Look for people to mentor and to help as they rediscover their own lights. Keep asking, *How can I help you?*

As my friend and colleague from the MG 100 Coaches group Morag Barrett, and her SkyeTeam colleagues, Eric Spencer, and Ruby Vesely, say in their book, *You, Me, We: Why We All Need a Friend at Work (and How to Show Up as One)*, "Every time you give, every time you pay it forward, you create a ripple in the world around you—in your people, in your clients and customers, in your suppliers and vendors, and in the communities in which you do business." They also go on to talk about being generous, stating, "Generosity is related to abundance but distinctly different. It's giving to others freely without the expectation of getting anything back in return or keeping count. It's akin to lighting someone else's candle. The act of lighting their candle doesn't diminish their own light; in fact it makes us all shine a little bit brighter." I love that! Look for ways to light someone else's candle, so that we can all shine brighter!

Coming from a mindset of abundance and generosity is a part of helping others in a way that feels great to each party, making each person stronger. I encourage you to think about how you can help others every day.

So many people helped me along the way to my present circumstances and success, and I will never forget those people. They are forever in my head and my heart and I continue to thank them every day. It's been quite a ride and it's still going! I think back about a situation that happened to me when I was in my mid-20s and searching for my next great adventure in my career.

One woman in particular, Kay M., went out of her way many years ago and took the time to help me prepare for my interviews to get one of my favorite jobs ever, at the Tribune Company. For that job, I also have Jen U., and Kris C., to thank for giving me the chance to build on something really great in a corporate structure that I had never been in before. (Since then, Kay and I have remained friends. I hired her to be a consultant at Tribune, and then eventually hired her to be my head of recruiting at MVP.)

Shortly thereafter came my boss, Luis L., who became an important and dear mentor and lifetime friend. He changed the game for me and taught me most of what I needed to be the leader that I am today. He led by example and taught me so much that I cannot even begin to imagine my life without his leadership and the lessons he imparted to me as a young executive. He's also the reason that I went to Kellogg for my MBA and for so many other amazing opportunities. He believed in me more than I believed in myself at the time. We remain close to this day, and I think of him with so much gratitude and appreciation for the way that he guided me, taught me, and changed the trajectory of my career. And there were so many others that made such a difference in my life along the way. As Dr. Mark Goulston, my dear friend and mentor whom we lost to a long battle with cancer this year, would say, this is a power thank you moment. So I say a big "power thank-you" to everyone on my journey for giving me a chance and believing in me.

So now, in turn, I want you to know that I believe in your dream. I ask that you continue to share your light and continue to do work that lights you up inside.

Your dreams are now becoming a reality and that, my dear reader, is how it should be. Keep this going, for the rest of your life.

It is my dream and hope that someday you too will love your job like I love my job. I'm beyond grateful to my clients; I feel so privileged to work with such amazing people who invite me into their hearts and their lives and share with me the most authentic and raw pieces of who they are. They have taught me so many things throughout the process of working with them and stretched me not only as a coach but as a human being.

It truly lights me up to watch my clients discover their light and uncover their passions. Because of them, I am a better coach today than I was yesterday. Because of them, my life and my work are rich, interesting, and full of meaning, and no two days are ever the same.

We are all in this together. I will say it again: I truly believe that when one person succeeds, we all succeed. It creates a ripple effect throughout the world, and I want to keep that positivity flowing for you, for me, and for every life we touch.

As I finished the final editing of the manuscript, my mom was in and out of the hospital, and we had to start her in the hospice protocol as a part of her end-of-life stages. Needless to say, I was and still am beyond devastated. I'd been staying up until all hours, writing on airplanes and editing like crazy from my sister's house in my hometown of Barrington, Illinois, as we navigated the end of life for my vivacious and amazing mother. It's been gut-wrenching, but I also recognize that it's part of the journey of life and such a sacred place of transition to be honored and accepted. Easier said than done when it is someone you love so dearly.

A few months ago, I was sobbing on the way to the airport and as I was boarding the airplane, I was greeted by the brightest light on the plane—a flight attendant named Paul. He greeted me with an enthusiastic smile and not only welcomed me onto the plane but told me how much he loved my scarf. (And those who know me know that scarves are kind of my thing!) Paul was lit up. He was exactly what I needed as I boarded the plane from Chicago to New York. Leaving my precious mom in Chicago and heading back to my family in New York was so hard, but I missed my husband and my kids and needed to take care of them, too. So with a heavy heart, I boarded the plane and Paul offered me a drink. I accepted, and then he looked at me with a wink and offered me a "double." I instantly declined, but boy did I appreciate the sentiment.

I went on to observe Paul as he went about his job as a flight attendant with the utmost enthusiasm and joy. It was so much fun to watch him work with such passion. This was exactly what I've been writing about. Maybe sometime in the future, I'll even be able to share Paul's story with you.

The point is that you never know whose life you will change by being lit up, being kind to others, and doing what you love. Your actions can change one person's day for the better, and then another and another, and eventually change the world.

I will end here with a "power thank-you" to you, my reader, for investing this time in yourself. I believe in you, and I am so grateful to be a part of your journey as you read and worked through the pages of this book.

Keep shining!
With love and light, always,
Mary

Exercises

To access digital downloads of these exercises and watch exclusive teachings, visit: MaryOlsonMenzel.com/Resources

Exercise 1

Finding Your Light

WHAT IS YOUR CURRENT EMPLOYMENT SITUATION?

1. Are you employed today? (Yes or no) _____
2. Do you have a vision of what your next job looks like? _____

   _____

   _____

   _____

   _____

3. How much money do you need to make to cover the basics?

   _____

4. How much do you realistically want to earn this year?

   _____

5. What kind of a work/life balance do you need? _____

   _____

   _____

_____

_____

WHAT MAKES YOU UNIQUE?

1. List three words that best describe what makes you unique. This could be in the context of work or at home. Think of qualities that you like about yourself.

    1. _____

    2. _____

    3. _____

2. Describe your sense of generosity. _____

    _____

    _____

    _____

3. Describe your sense of humor. _____

    _____

    _____

    _____

4. Describe yourself as a problem solver, or someone who can get things done with efficiency. _____

    _____

    _____

    _____

5. Describe your abilities around kindness, empathy, and care.

    _____

    _____

    _____

    _____

6. Describe how you embrace a positive attitude in work.

_____

_____

_____

_____

7. Describe how you use your intuition at work.

_____

_____

_____

_____

8. Describe how your listening skills enhance your performance.

_____

_____

_____

_____

9. What qualities might set you apart from others at work or home?

_____

_____

_____

_____

10. List three things you are most proud of in either your personal and/or professional life. This can include accomplishments, activities, skills, behaviors, and so on.

1. _____

2. _____

3. _____

If you have a hard time identifying this, ask a friend or a family member. These qualities typically come so easily to you that you might not even think of them, but they do lead you to your light.

WHAT ARE YOUR INTERESTS AND HOBBIES?

List things that interest you and keep your light on. This could include anything from mentoring junior employees at your organization to running the charity 5K. Do you have a side hustle, a passion you're doing in the hours when you're not working (for example, photography, art, traveling, playing an instrument, speaking another language, hiking, boating, or yoga)? _____

_____

_____

_____

_____

_____

_____

_____

_____

WHAT'S ON YOUR BUCKET LIST?

Put together a list of things you have done in the past that you now look back on with joy and gratitude. And then create a bucket list of what you would like to do in the future. For example, when I was younger, I was passionate about scuba diving and have had the amazing opportunity to dive in five different countries and many beautiful locations around the world. As I've gotten older, I've become a little bit more risk-averse and so the scuba has shifted to hiking. One of my current bucket list items is to travel with my family to all seven continents. *Another bucket list item of mine was to write this book.*

There are no rules when it comes to your bucket list. No matter how big or how small, if it's something you've done or something you'd like to do, put it on this list. Have fun with this and let yourself enjoy the process!

GRATITUDE LIST

_____

_____

_____

_____

_____

_____

_____

_____

FUTURE BUCKET LIST

_____

_____

_____

_____

_____

_____

WHAT ARE YOUR PASSIONS AND DREAMS?

What did you dream of doing as a child?

_____

_____

_____

_____

_____

1. What aspects of your past or current job(s) are related to your childhood dreams? _____

   _____

   _____

   _____

   _____

2. What are your dreams now, and how have they changed since you were a child? _____

   _____

_____

_____

_____

_____

3. What are you most passionate about right now? _____

_____

_____

_____

_____

4. What makes you the happiest right now? _____

_____

_____

_____

_____

Exercise 2

Create Your Daily Light Log

Make a list of all the things that bring you joy. These don't have to be big things; you can start with the simple pleasures in life, such as enjoying a good cup of coffee. It can be your dog greeting you with kisses after your morning run. It might even be a partner, child, or friend giving you a much-needed hug. Even the pleasure of crossing items off your to-do list can bring joy and satisfaction to your day. Whatever it is, list it, and keep paying attention throughout your day to anything that brings a smile to your face!

_____

_____

_____

_____

_____

_____

_____

_____

_____

_____

_____

_____

_____

_____

_____

_____

_____

_____

_____

_____

_____

Exercise 3

Creating Your Narrative

Now that you understand the importance of your story, let's get started on creating it. Answer the questions below to the best of your ability. Think carefully about the path you have traveled and what it means to you. Additionally, focus on which parts of your story highlight your strengths and character and what aspects of your story might be compelling to a future employer.

High School: (or earlier)   List two or three jobs or experiences that you had that might have led you to your career path.

   1. _____

   _____

2. _____

3. _____

College: Why did you choose to attend a particular college? _____

_____

How did you decide on a major or minor? _____

_____

Did you change your major? _____
Attend graduate school? _____
What inspired you to make these decisions at this time in your life?

_____

What were your motivations for making these choices? _____

_____

_____

_____

_____

Alternate Path: We all follow different paths, and there is no wrong answer here. If you didn't go to college, that is a part of your story. What was your alternate path when you finished high school? _____

_____

_____

_____

_____

_____

_____

_____

_____

_____

Employment Experience: Answer the following questions for two favorite jobs that you've had and for your current job. (If you're not currently working, you can answer for a third past job.)

Job 1   What were your job title and job responsibilities? _____

_____

_____

_____

_____

_____

_____

How did you get the job? _____

_____

_____

_____

_____

_____

Did you enjoy your work? In other words, did the work "light you up"?

_____

_____

_____

_____

_____

If not, what parts do you want to avoid in your next job? _____

_____

_____

_____

_____

_____

What new skills did you learn? _____

_____

_____

_____

_____

_____

What did you learn about yourself? _____

_____

_____

_____

_____

_____

What contributions do you feel you made to the organization and how did those contributions make you feel at the end of the day? _____

_____

_____

_____

_____

_____

Why did you leave? _____

_____

_____

_____

_____

_____

What other skills would you like to learn in the next job? (for your own thought process) _____

_____

_____

_____

_____

_____

Job 2   What were your job title and responsibilities? _____

_____

_____

_____

_____

_____

How did you get the job? _____

_____

_____

_____

_____

Did you enjoy your work? In other words, did the work "light you up"?

_____

_____

_____

_____

If not, what parts do you want to avoid in your next job? _____

_____

_____

_____

_____

What new skills did you learn? _____

_____

_____

_____

_____

_____

What did you learn about yourself? _____

_____

_____

_____

_____

_____

What contributions do you feel you made to the organization and
how did those contributions make you feel at the end of the day? _____

_____

_____

_____

_____

_____

Why did you leave? _____

_____

_____

_____

_____

_____

What other skills would you like to learn in the next job? (for your own thought process) _____

_____

_____

_____

_____

_____

Current Job   What were your job title and responsibilities? _____

_____

_____

_____

_____

How did you get the job? _____

_____

_____

_____

_____

Did you enjoy your work? In other words, did the work "light you up"?

_____

_____

_____

_____

_____

If not, what parts do you want to avoid in your next job? _____

_____

_____

_____

_____

_____

What new skills did you learn? _____

_____

_____

_____

_____

What did you learn about yourself? _____

_____

_____

_____

_____

What contributions do you feel you made to the organization and how did those contributions make you feel at the end of the day? ____

_____

_____

_____

_____

Why did you leave? _____

_____

_____

_____

_____

_____

What other skills would you like to learn in the next job? (for your own thought process) _____

_____

_____

_____

_____

These answers are for your eyes only. You will use the information to craft your story, and being totally honest with yourself will help you to further zoom in on where you want to go.

There are no wrong answers. Do not judge yourself on where you've been. Honor your path and recognize why you made the decisions that have led you to where you are today. Pay attention to when you listened to your heart and when you were the happiest. Also, notice which of your decisions and experiences led to feeling unhappy or unfulfilled. There is so much to learn from this exercise besides creating a personal narrative, so take your time and answer each question carefully.

Now, let's look back at everything you have written.

What patterns do you see? _____

_____

_____

_____

_____

_____

_____

_____

_____

_____

What kind of narrative is emerging? _____

_____

_____

_____

_____

_____

_____

_____

Go back to the questions. Where can you go deeper? _____

_____

_____

_____

_____

_____

_____

Are there things that you can now answer a little more clearly as you revisit the questions and look at the bigger picture? _____

_____

_____

_____

_____

_____

What are you learning about yourself along the way? _____

_____

_____

_____

_____

_____

_____

Once you have answered the questions above, put an asterisk next to or circle those answers that highlight your strengths or your character the most. Then do the same for the answers that are most relevant to your current job search. Use the selected answers as the key points to create your narrative. Once you've identified the key points you want to include in your narrative, weave in personal stories to make it more interesting and compelling.

Prospects, Pivots, and Passions

Use the tables below to record your prospects, pivots, and passions, following the guidelines given here.

Prospects

The first step is to create your target list of companies that *you* are interested in. On this list, you will start to identify companies or organizations that you may have admired for a while or that you may have recently found intriguing. This will involve a fair amount of research to determine which companies are worth pursuing and which companies might be the right cultural fit for you.

Pivots

A "pivot" is a conscious change in strategy to a different industry, a different role, or a complete change into a new field. It usually takes a little more thought and effort than a prospect, but most of the time it's worth it, when you're ready for a change.

This is where you're ready to take a new perspective, or a slight shift. These are companies or organizations that you may have admired for a while or have a new interest in, where you could possibly imagine taking your existing skills and moving them into a slightly different industry or organization.

Passions

Under your "passions" column, you will want to include companies that align with your passions or that might enable you to do something that you're truly passionate about. You can refer to your "light log" to identify what some of those passions are.

Prospects: _____

_____

_____

_____

_____

Pivots:

Passions:

Recruiter Connections:

Recruiter Name	Connection to Recruiter	Last Date of Contact/ Details	Pertinent Information About Recruiter	Next Steps

Prospects, Pivots, Passions: Making the Connections

Company Name	Prospect, Pivot or Passion	Connection to Company	Last Date of Contact/ Details	Pertinent Information About Company	Next Steps

Checklist for Interview Readiness

- Make sure you have a strong knowledge of the industry and the company you are interviewing with ahead of time. Do your research; get to know the company from every perspective and every angle.
- Google the profiles of the people you will be interviewing with.
- Check out their LinkedIn profiles and make sure you know who they are, what they've done, and if you have any mutual connections.
- Go back to the list you made earlier and practice selling your strengths. What are your distinguishing traits and qualifications that will benefit the recruiter, hiring manager, and company if they hire you?
- Make the effort to sell yourself and tell your story in an authentic way and let your light and passion shine so that people will remember you.
- Always use examples from real life. This will add color and credibility to your conversations.
- Have a list of thoughtful questions prepared to ask them. Listen closely to what they have to say and make sure that your questions are relevant and appropriate for the interview.
- Reconfirm what they say at the end of the conversation, and make sure you understand next steps and what to do to follow up.

Behavioral-Based Interview Questions

Give an example of a goal you reached and tell me how you achieved it.

_____

_____

_____

_____

_____

_____

_____

Give an example of a goal you didn't meet and how you handled it.

_____

_____

_____

_____

_____

Describe a stressful situation at work and how you handled it.

_____

_____

_____

_____

_____

Share an example of how you were able to motivate employees or co-workers in a difficult time.

_____

_____

_____

_____

_____

Emotional Intelligence (EI)

EI is the capacity to identify and understand the impact of your feelings regarding thoughts, decisions, behavior, and performance at work in addition to a greater understanding of others, and how to engage, respond, motivate, and connect with them.

Tell me about a time when you felt confident in your abilities and your work. Why did you feel confident? What was the result?

_____

_____

_____

_____

_____

_____

Think of a situation you faced where you felt frustrated or stressed at work. Why were you frustrated? What was the impact you had on the other people who were involved?

_____

_____

_____

_____

_____

_____

What is an example of something that isn't one of your strengths? What have you done to accommodate this challenge?

_____

_____

_____

_____

_____

_____

Tell me about a time when you faced a significant change. What was the nature of the change and how did you react?

_____

_____

_____

_____

_____

_____

How would your current or previous co-workers, supervisor, and staff describe your communication and interpersonal style? Give an example or two.

_____

_____

_____

_____

_____

Think of a challenging working relationship you've had. What was your part in the difficulty, and what was their part? Tell me about the person and your interactions with them. What did you do to address the relationship or make it more successful?

_____

_____

_____

_____

_____

Tell me about a time your ability to appropriately use empathy turned a tricky situation around. Describe how you were able to transform it into something positive.

_____

_____

_____

_____

_____

_____

Flexibility

Describe a time that you had to be open minded and adjust to a new structure, process, or culture.

_____

_____

_____

Describe a time when you had to adapt your style while working with a group of people.

_____

_____

_____

_____

_____

_____

Describe a time you had to change your point of view to consider new information or a change in priorities.

_____

_____

_____

_____

_____

_____

Give a specific example of how you have helped create an environment where different perspectives are valued, encouraged, and supported. What did you do? What was the outcome?

_____

_____

_____

_____

_____

_____

Creativity

Give a specific example of what you have done to encourage innovation to accomplish the strategic goals and objectives of your organization. What did you do? What was the outcome?

_____

_____

_____

_____

_____

Describe a time you made a major sacrifice to achieve an important goal. Was it worth it?

_____

_____

_____

_____

_____

_____

Many internal and external factors can impact an organization. Give a specific example of what you have done when the organization's priorities changed quickly. What was the situation? What did you do? What was the outcome or result? What obstacles and challenges did you face?

_____

_____

_____

_____

_____

_____

Goal Setting and Accomplishments

Describe a time when you set a goal for yourself and did not achieve it. What happened? Was there anything you could have done differently?

_____

_____

_____

_____

_____

_____

_____

Successes: Give an example of an important goal you achieved and how you accomplished that goal.

_____

_____

_____

_____

_____

_____

_____

Challenges: Describe a time when you set a goal for yourself and did not achieve it. What were the ramifications of your failure to achieve your goal?

_____

_____

_____

_____

_____

_____

_____

Processes: Describe how you set your goals and how you measure your accomplishments. Did you achieve your goals? If not, why not? Tell me about a major project you recently finished. Specifically, how did you set the goals and track your progress?

_____

_____

_____

_____

_____

_____

_____

_____

Challenges: Describe a time you were given a goal that you believed would be impossible to attain. How did you handle it?

_____

_____

_____

_____

_____

_____

_____

_____

Relationship Management

How do you go about building relationships with key stakeholders to help get the job done?

_____

_____

_____

_____

_____

_____

Give an example of a time when you were able to build rapport quickly with someone in your organization.

_____

_____

_____

_____

_____

_____

_____

Describe a time you collaborated with others in different areas or cross-departmentally, to determine courses of action to achieve mutual goals.

_____

_____

_____

_____

_____

_____

Describe a time when you successfully gained the trust of a client, key stakeholder, or someone at work.

_____

_____

_____

_____

_____

_____

Describe a time when you were willing to disagree with another person in order to build a positive outcome.

_____

_____

_____

_____

_____

_____

Give an example of how you worked with a difficult direct report or colleague. How did you handle the situation? Were you able to get along?

_____

_____

_____

_____

_____

_____

Problem-Solving

Give an example of a time when you actively defined several solutions to a single problem. Which solution did you choose and why?

_____

_____

_____

_____

_____

_____

Give an example of a time when you used fact-finding skills to solve a problem.

_____

_____

_____

_____

_____

_____

_____

Describe a problem you solved that best demonstrates your analytical abilities.

_____

_____

_____

_____

_____

_____

Project Management

Describe a successful program or project that you developed where you had to coordinate and manage a diverse team of people to achieve deliverables.

_____

_____

_____

_____

_____

What processes are important when implementing a new program across multiple business units?

_____

_____

_____

_____

_____

_____

_____

Potential Interview Questions

These questions come from a Harvard Study.

What is your favorite kind of ice cream, or other sweet treat?

_____

_____

_____

_____

_____

_____

How would your parents describe you when you were twelve?

_____

_____

_____

_____

_____

_____

What's the one thing you'll never be as good at as others?

_____

_____

_____

_____

_____

_____

How would your friends describe you in three words?

1. _____

2. _____

3. _____

Describe something that you should start doing, do more of, and do less of.

_____

_____

_____

_____

_____

_____

_____

Please tell me about three failures you've had and what you learned from them.

1. _____

2. _____

3. _____

Leadership Signature

Create a leadership signature and build cultures of excellence. It starts with the alignment of the following:

What is your north star? Think of this as your top leadership declaration. What is the essence of who you are as a leader and as an organization?

What is your mission? Your mission should be big-picture, long-term, and meaningful. It's your *why*.

What is your goal? This is less about values and more about the bottom line. It's actionable and measurable.

What is your value proposition? Prioritize the top values that you hold dearest in your role and for your team. What lights you up?

_____

_____

_____

What is your promise? What is the promise you offer to your employees and to your clients/customers?

_____

_____

_____

_____

_____

_____

What is your mantra? What do you say to yourself and your team every day to ensure that your culture and your leadership are inspiring?

_____

_____

_____

_____

_____

_____

Remember, this is a reflective exercise for you alone. Refer to it regularly, both as a reminder to yourself and to see if anything has shifted or evolved. Keep yourself accountable!

Set a Framework for Success

"Mad Libs"

This fun and thought-provoking Mad Libs–style exercise gets the creative juices flowing and helps to clarify expectations and set intentions. It's a great individual or team exercise to do during the first few months of your employment. Plus, it's an enjoyable way to get to know your team and get them all in sync.

"Filling in the blanks" enables a team to identify where their professional goals align with their company's goals. These don't have to line up perfectly, but it's important to recognize the distinction and use that information accordingly. As mentioned, you can do this for yourself and also if you have a team. If you do have a team, use this as a group exercise, to help get everyone to "buy in" right out of the gate.

Individual Goals   My goal for my work is:

_____

_____

_____

_____

_____

The biggest reason I chose this is:

_____

_____

_____

_____

_____

_____

Previously, the three things I was most proud of was:

1. _____
   _____

2. _____
   _____

3. _____
   _____

I also faced three big challenges in the form of:

1. _____

_____

2. _____

_____

3. _____

_____

What would achieving this goal mean for me? For my life? For my business?

_____

_____

_____

_____

_____

_____

One behavior I must eliminate to achieve this is:

_____

_____

_____

_____

_____

One behavior I must cultivate to help me achieve this is:

_____

_____

_____

_____

_____

My bucket list wish for my work is (dream big here!):

_____

_____

_____

_____

_____

Once you've gotten clarity on your personal goals, look at what you want to achieve in the workplace. If you have a team, how can you be just as intentional about driving results for yourself and your team? Get very clear on what success looks like so you can create a plan to help you achieve it. Remember, you are not alone. Include your teammates and colleagues in this planning as well. Understand each team member's motivations and strengths and assign them tasks accordingly to help move forward together.

Team/Organizational Goals   My team's goals for the business are:

_____

_____

_____

_____

_____

The biggest reason we chose this is:

_____

_____

_____

_____

_____

In the past, the three things we were most proud of were:

_____

_____

_____

_____

As a team, we also faced three big challenges in the form of:

_____

_____

_____

_____

What would achieving these goals mean for our team? Our business?

_____

_____

_____

_____

One behavior we must eliminate in our team/culture to achieve this is:

_____

_____

_____

_____

One behavior we must cultivate in our team/culture to help us achieve this is:

_____

_____

_____

_____

_____

_____

Our bucket list wish for our team is (dream big here!):

_____

_____

_____

_____

_____

_____

Now that you have reflected on and put intention into your goals, start to create a strategy for how to make it happen. Try not to get overwhelmed. Break it into baby steps and tackle some every day. This is how we make progress! Set up bimonthly or quarterly meetings to check in on progress and support each other in your shared resolutions. All you need is an hour, a whiteboard, and an open mind to set a framework for shared success.

Gratitude and Goals

Consider organizing a Gratitude and Goals meeting, where every team member can look their colleagues in the eyes, tell them what they appreciate about them, and give examples about how they have had a positive impact on their work this year. After they've gone around the room expressing gratitude, it's time to brainstorm one thing that each team member can do to help achieve team goals and create success for the rest of the year.

What's your focus now?

_____

_____

_____

_____

Are you headed in the right direction?

_____

_____

_____

_____

Where do you want to be at this time next year?

_____

_____

_____

_____

Those big plans, goals, and benchmarks you started planning for in the last chapter will benefit from your own review of what's been working, and where improvements can be made. Tweak what you can now so you end each year on a high!

ABCs This simple exercise is something I hope you will do with your family, your friends, and your team on a regular basis. This is something that you can always come back to on a regular basis, to keep you motivated and on course at any stage of your career journey.

Achievements: What have you done this year that hit or exceeded your goals? What are you most proud of?

_____

_____

_____

_____

_____

_____

_____

Blessings: What people, things, or situations in your life and your workplace are you grateful for?

_____

_____

_____

_____

_____

_____

_____

Commitments: What will you commit to that will get you to success for the year?

_____

_____

_____

_____

_____

_____

_____

Acknowledgments

As I HAVE mentioned before, it takes a village to write and publish a book. I could not have done any of this without the help of so many amazing people.

First and foremost, my profound gratitude goes to both of my parents, Robert and Veronica, and my siblings, Jimmy, Sandy, Connie, John, Robert, and Tricia. Without our blended family dynamics and your love and support, I would not have grown into the person that I am today. To Sandy, for taking care of me and being the best big sister since "day one," thank you for your easygoing nature, ongoing support, and enthusiasm for every endeavor. To John, for being the calm in any storm for me; your unique combination of deep faith and sense of humor always grounds me and your hugs make me feel so loved and safe, always. To Robert, for our Christmas tree decorating in Chicago, your willingness to be my airport Uber at any time, and for your never-ending supply of Chex Mix. And especially, to Tricia, my "right arm," my sounding board, my partner in so many life adventures, for your early edits and for always being there for me, in all ways; what on earth would I do without you by my side on this journey?

To my husband, Dan, thank you for your constant support and encouragement as I have been locked up writing and editing through nights, weekends, and vacations. To my amazing kids, my stepkids,

Sam and Connor, and my son, Christopher—you three have taught me more about patience, life, and love than any parenting book ever could have taught me in a lifetime.

To my business partners and colleagues, and especially to my MVP team both past and present, Michelle, Cindy, Randy, Kathleen, Kathryn, Clare, Laura, Kay, Kate, Mel, Lizzy, Eve, Georges, Kim and Tricia. Without you all supporting me and working to keep our clients happy every step of the way, I could not have done any of this.

To Elizabeth DelGiudice, for being with me every step of the way, for being my sounding board and for being so patient with me through every edit and every draft from the very beginning. For not only cheering me on through all of the ups and downs but also anticipating and preparing for my next move, even before I think about it myself— and for all of your assistance and hard work in helping to make my dream of being an author come true. You are the true MVP and I do not know what I would do without you!!!

To my MVP-SPARK business partner, Mel Shahbazian, for your endless creativity, support, and inspiration. Thank you for showing me how to have fun, create balance, and be present in the moments, regardless of who we are, who we are working with, or what we are doing. Working with you is the best and "gratitude is everything"! Thank you, I'm so grateful for you!

To Kate Winter, whom I've known since our Tribune days, for rolling with the changes in direction and looking at things from an analytical perspective that helps me to pause and think before I leap into action using both logic and grace.

To Eve Hoeltgen, for sharing your instincts, and insights, and also for your diligence and attention in keeping our complicated schedules organized at every turn, all with a big smile on your face.

And I'm so grateful to my business partners, Diane, Mary and the team at Ragan Communications. And to my trusted colleagues, consultants, and advisors, Georges O. R. Chakar, Ashley Zink, Victoria Labalme, Beverley Delay, Evan Schapiro, Lilian Ohman, and Deborah S. Marquardt, who are in my corner nonstop, sharing their own talents, light, wisdom, and advice on a regular basis. Without these people and so many more surrounding me, my light would not be as bright as it is and I would not be having nearly as much fun.

To my bosses and mentors throughout my entire career, at Channel 6, CPS, Software Architects, Tribune, WGN, HSK, and Ascend who taught me both what to do and what not to do to create lasting success. To my favorite professors at both Illinois State and Kellogg/Northwestern. To my classmates from BHS and in both undergrad and b-school, some of whom are still my best friends, Three Cuties in a Row, Smokin Hot Tribune Mamas, Team B and PL7.

To my dearest friends from all over the world but mostly from Larchmont, New York, Chicago, and Southern California—you know who you are—I couldn't do this life without any of you; your friendship and support means the world to me! I am so grateful for each and every one of you and I can't wait to celebrate with you all!

To the whole team at Wiley, including Cheryl Segura, Amanda Pyne, and so many others working behind the scenes to make this book come to life, and most of all to Cheryl, for believing in me and staying connected until the "right time" came for us to work together! To Sunnye Collins, for your edits and your smiles as I navigated our work with edits and more edits, and to Amy Handy, Sharmila Srinivasan and Sangeetha Suresh, for even more copyedits. To the Book Highlight team, especially Peter Knox, Brian Morrison, Alana Whitman and Margret Wiggins for making this all come together so seamlessly. To Anne Barthel at Hay House for connecting me with Cheryl so many years ago. To my attorney, Matthew Savare, for jumping in whenever needed and guiding me in the right direction. To the late Dr. Mark Goulston and to the powerhouse, Marshall Goldsmith and all of the MG 100 Coaches, Morag Barrett, Ruth Gotian, Todd Cherches, Tricia Gorton, Chester Elton, Doug Guthrie, Jennifer Fondrevay, Evelyn Rodstein, Richard Osibanjo, Macarena Ybarra, Eddie Turner, John Sviokla, John Baldoni, and so many others who jumped in to amplify, elevate, and support me on this journey. And to Stacy Robin, for introducing me to Mark and Matt in the first place.

To Leah Komaiko, for being an integral part of coaching me and helping me find my true voice; to Nikki Marie Bruhn, for your spiritual counsel and guidance and for helping me continue to raise my vibration; and to Debbie Pincus, for telling me so many years ago, "Just start writing"!

To every person, friend and client mentioned in the book, thank you for allowing me to share your incredible stories with the world! And to every amazing person who believed in me and endorsed this book, I am honored.

I am forever grateful to every client who has ever trusted me with their career and with their hearts. Thank you for your time, your hard work, and your investment in yourself and your future. You are the reason for this book!

About the Author

Mary Olson-Menzel has over 30 years of leadership experience across media, tech, healthcare, and many other industries globally. She is the founder and CEO of MVP Executive Development (www .mvpexec.com), a national leadership, coaching, and organizational management consultancy with offices in New York, Connecticut, and Illinois. Clients range from Fortune 500 companies to start-ups with a broad reach of industries from fintech to football (the NFL). As a seasoned executive leadership coach, Mary works with both companies and individuals to unlock the potential that improves business performance and catalyzes growth. Her coaching methods bring a fresh lens to business and a perspective that nurtures teamwork and helps drive results through grace, empathy, and "Humane Leadership."

Before starting her own company in 2012, Mary was a partner at two leading global executive search firms. She also spent a decade at Tribune Company in Chicago as national managing director, leading a national team of human capital professionals. This is where her understanding and expertise of recruiting and coaching was honed. She worked closely with 20 newspapers, 27 television stations, and hundreds of digital assets across the country to attract and retain the best and the brightest.

In her early years, Mary worked in both the tech space and media and entertainment, where she started her career as a television reporter. Her innate curiosity and ability to connect with people paved the way for her life's work: helping leaders at all levels channel what "lights them up" and inspires them into more fulfilling and successful personal and professional journeys.

She is a member of the Marshall Goldsmith 100 Coaches, which brings together the world's leading executive coaches, consultants, speakers, authors, iconic leaders, and entrepreneurs. She is also a part of the Kellogg Executive Women's Network (KEWN). Mary also volunteers for Northwestern University's Alumni Admissions Council and for other various charities in her local community.

Mary earned her MBA from Northwestern University's Kellogg School of Business and a bachelor's degree in communications and public relations from Illinois State University.

Mary currently lives in Westchester, New York, with her husband, three kids, and their goldendoodle, Wrigley.

Notes

Chapter 2

1. https://www.inc.com/justin-bariso/neuroscience-says-1-simple-habit-boosts-brain-connectivity-learning-memory

Chapter 3

1. https://news.harvard.edu/gazette/story/2020/02/men-better-than-women-at-self-promotion-on-job-leading-to-inequities/

Chapter 4

1. https://www.linkedin.com/pulse/must-know-job-website-statistics-your-online-recruitment-/
2. https://www.ere.net/articles/why-you-cant-get-a-job-recruiting-explained-by-the-numbers
3. https://teamstage.io/resume-statistics/
4. https://www.theladders.com/career-advice/ats-what-is-it-and-how-does-it-impact-hiring
5. https://www.linkedin.com/pulse/5-mindblowing-linkedin-statistics-job-search-harshad-bhagwat-1e/

6. https://www.linkedin.com/pulse/your-linkedin-profile-picture-matters-more-than-you-think-rotko/

7. https://www.linkedin.com/pulse/your-linkedin-profile-picture-matters-more-than-you-think-rotko/

8. https://www.cnbc.com/2023/01/13/96percent-of-workers-are-looking-for-a-new-job-in-2023.html#:~:text=Personal%20Finance-,96%25%20of%20workers%20are%20looking%20for%20a%20new%20job%20in,know%20before%20you%20job%20hop&text=A%20whopping%2096%25%20of%20workers,recent%20report%20by%20Monster.com)

Chapter 5

1. https://www.pewresearch.org/social-trends/2023/03/30/how-americans-view-their-jobs/

2. https://www.gallup.com/cliftonstrengths/en/254033/strengthsfinder.aspx

Chapter 8

1. https://www.statista.com/statistics/1418354/recruitment-methods-us/

2. https://harrykraemer.org/2016/07/26/on-balance/

Chapter 9

1. Marianne Williamson, *A Return to Love: Reflections on the Principles of "A Course in Miracles."*

Chapter 10

1. https://www.strongdm.com/blog/employee-onboarding-statistics

Chapter 14

1. https://positivepsychology.com/neuroscience-of-gratitude/

Index

A

Abundance mindset, 136
Accomplishments, 92–93
Achievements, Blessings,
	Commitments (ABCs),
	131, 181–182
Advisory board, assembly, 16
All Dreams on Deck (Cage), 24
Always be connecting
	(ABC), 109
Answers, trust, 13–14
Anxiety, reduction, 123
Applicant tracking system
	(ATS), résumé
	(optimization), 33
Authenticity, impact, 37

B

Barrett, Morag, 136
Behavioral-based interview
	questions, 160–161
	preparation, 89
Body/mind/spirit,
	refreshing, 122
Body, movement, 123
Branson, Richard, 28
Breaths, usage, 86, 130
Bucket list, identification,
	15, 142, 143
Business
	running, administrative
	tasks, 58
	starting, 70, 79

C

Cage, Jeremy, 24
Career
  building, goal, 39
  crossroads, 56
  exit, meaning, 4–5
  focus, absence, 72
  goals, 101–102
  journey, 19, 75
  lighting, 3
  magic, 11
  pivot, 25, 78–79
  problem, 56–57
  role, consideration, 97–98
  trajectory, change, 64
Challenges, 167, 168
Charity, importance, 77
Client
  lives, understanding/
    knowledge, 72–73
  onboarding playbooks, team
    design, 103
Clinton, Michael, 120
Coaches, impact, 1–2
Companies, identification/
    admiration, 62
Compassion, life lessons, 79
Connections, making, 67–69
Contact, making, 51–53
Contingency recruiting firms,
    hiring, 50
Corporate recruiters, TheLadder
    .com study, 32
Covid-19 pandemic, impact, 37
Creativity
  exercises, 165–166
  innovation, combination, 92
Cultural fit, 62

D

Daily light log, creation,
    17–18, 144
Decision-making journey,
    initiation, 71
Destiny, control, 108–109
Development, character-
    istics, 107
Dreams, 75
  following, 39
  identification, 16, 143–144
  motion, 76
  problem, 119–120
  realization, 137

E

Elton, Chester, 130
Emmons, Robert, 130
Emotional intelligence (EI),
    90–91, 161–164
Empathetic leadership,
    123–124
Empathy, life lessons, 79
Employee engagement/
    connection, opportuni-
    ties (creation), 101–102
Employers
  humane leaders,
    presence, 102
  negotiation, 98
  search, 37

Employment
   experience, 28–30, 147–156
   gap, list, 36–37
   situation, analysis,
     14, 139–140
Exercises, 139
Experience
   combining, 78
   impact, 5–6, 20–21

F
Fear, 84
"Filling in the blanks," 116
Financial needs/goals,
    balance, 43–44
First impression,
    importance, 104
Fletcher, Emily, 130
Flexibility, concept,
    91, 164–165
Forward momentum,
    creation, 107
Fox, Michael J. (gratitude),
    128

G
Gates, Bill, 28
Generosity, abundance
    (contrast), 136
Gig economy, side hustle
    (acceptance), 120
Gittens Ottley, Sonja, 103
Giving back, impact, 77
Global crisis, safe position
    (maintenance), 47

Goals
   accomplishments, 166–168
   aim, 77
   creation, 114
   exercises, 180–182
   focus, 104, 125
   identification, 115,
     174, 176–178
   setting, 92–93, 166–168
   types, 116–118
   writing, 113
Goldsmith, Marshall, 129, 134
Gostick, Adrian, 130
Goulston, Mark, 131–132,
    137
Grace, 119
Gratitude
   abundance, 130
   exercises, 180–182
   expression/receiving,
     130–131
   focus, 125
   list, 142–143
   practice, 127
   steps, 131
Gratitude and Goals meeting,
    organization, 125, 180
*Gratitude Habit: A 90-Day
    Journal to a More
    Grateful Life* (Elton/
    Gostick), 130
Greatness, shades, 4
Growth, support (advice),
    109
Gut check, 121–122

H

Handwritten thank-you
　　notes, usage, 96
Happiness, factors
　　(identification), 16
Hardships, overcoming,
　　25–26
Hard skills, impact, 3
Heart, light (appearance), 8
Help
　asking, 48–49
　offering, 45–48
Honesty, benefit, 99
Humane leadership, 123–124

I

Ikigai (a reason to live), 65–66
Individual goals, 116
Influence, opportunity, 97
Informational coffee meetings,
　　scheduling, 51
Innate curiosity, 25
Inner light, impact, 2–3
Inner voice
　guiding, 67
　listening, 84
Insight Timer app, usage, 123
Interests/hobbies, identification,
　　15, 141–142
Interviewer
　connection, 89
　questioning, 95–96
Interviews
　conducting, 12
　difference, 96
　directing, 86
　phase, entry, 84–85

preparation, 88, 94
purpose, 23
questions, 172–173
readiness, checklist,
　　88–90, 160
skills, practice, 85
success, 83

J

Job
　acceptance, 101
　application, 72
　example, 21
　history, description, 19
　issues, 98
　landing, 83
　negotiation, 99
　opportunity, 68
　pivot, 41
　satisfaction, 40
　search, 35, 39, 63–64
　　résumé, importance, 32
Jobs, Steve, 28
Journey
　embarking, 6–7
　employer interest, 20
　initiation, 71
　learning journey, 108
　path
　　alternates, 28
　　honoring, 29
　plans/occurrences, 24–25
　twists/turns, 23–26
Joy
　factors, 17
　finding, 135
　selection, 55

Just Listen: Discover the Secret to Getting Through to Absolutely (Goulston), 131

K
Key performance indicators (KPIs), 110
Kindness, life lessons, 79
Kraemer, Harry, 72
Kumar, Snehal, 127

L
Labalme, Victoria, 96
Leadership
  DNA, 114–115
  example, 73–74
  inventory, usage, 114–115
  signature, 173–175
Leading with Gratitude: Eight Leadership Practices for Extraordinary Business Results (Elton/ Gostick), 130
Learning journey, 108
Life
  creation, 6
  exploration, 41
  surprises, 121, 129
  survival, 128
Light
  absence, 57
  attention, 134
  concept, exploration, 66–67
  daily light log, creation, 17–18

disappearance, 5
finding
  example, 14–16
  exercise, 139–144
identification, 1
ignition, 11
innate superpower, 47
inner light, impact, 2–3
log, creation, 17–18
need, 7–8
LinkedIn, growth, 35
LinkedIn profile
  building, recommendations, 35–36
  importance, 34–38
  recruiter examination, 33–34
  scanability, 34
Loved ones, connection, 123

M
Mad Libs, usage, 115, 118, 175–180
Marketing, 78–79
Marketplace, uncertainty, 46
Massage, benefit, 123
Meeting
  importance, 104
  scheduling, 53
  video meeting, login, 87
Mind, change (allowance), 21–22
Mindset/energy, importance, 11
Mission
  identification, 115, 174
  writing, 113

Morning meditation,
    usage, 122–123

N
Narrative
    creation, 27, 145–156
    development, 20–21
    fine-tuning, 84
Network
    connecting, practice, 47–48
    control, 109
    growth, 68
    tapping, 45
North star, identification,
    115, 118, 174

O
Onboarding
    playbooks, team designs, 103
    process, 102
Optimism, gratitude (link), 127
Organizations
    goals, 116–118, 178–180
    identification/admiration, 62

P
Parents, origin story 5–6
Passions, 61, 65–68, 75–78
    exercise, 156–159
    identification, 16, 143–144
    increase, 79–81
    purpose, balance, 43–44
Patience, life lessons, 79
Pause, power, 85–86
Paycheck, equivalences, 8

Personal experience, demon-
    stration, 26
Personal stories, usage, 26
Phone screens, 85
Pivots, 25, 61, 63–65, 68, 75–79
    change, 120–121
    example, 70–73
    exercise, 157–160
    increase, 79–81
    intention, 64
Plans/occurrences, 24–25
Plan/strategy, creation, 43
Power Thank You, 131, 132
Presentation, improvement,
    111
Priorities
    change, 69
    focus, 104
Problem-solving, usage,
    94, 170–171
Processes, 167–168
Professional brand,
    building, 35
Project management, usage,
    94, 171–172
Promise/mantra, identification,
    115, 175
Prospects, Pivots, Passions
    (Three Ps), 61, 63–68
    examples, 69–70
    exercises, 156–159
    target list organiza-
    tions, 71–72
Purpose/passion, balance,
    43–44

Q

Qualified candidate, hiring, 12
Quiet confidence, 86–87

R

Real business/responsibility, 6
Recruiters
    connections, 159
    interaction, 49–50
Recruitment process, time/
        money (company
        expenditure), 103
Relationships
    building, 62
    management, 93, 168–170
    solidification, 102–103
Results, delivery, 26
Résumé
    error, impact, 33
    gaps, overcoming, 31
    impact, 19–20
    importance, 32–34
    optimization, 33
Retained recruiting firms,
        hiring, 50–51
Review, Reach, Recreate (three
        Rs), 109–111
*Risk Forward: Embrace the
        Unknown and Unlock
        Your Hidden Genius*
        (Labalme), 97
*Roar: into the second half of your
        life (Before It's Too Late)*
        (Clinton), 120
Rock The Room®
        (Labalme), 96–97

S

Search engine optimization
        (SEO), 34
Self-assessment, 114–115
Self-balance, creation, 122
Self-care, importance, 121–123
Shahbazian, Mel, 114,
        115, 131
Shining, 84, 96, 135, 138
Short-term goal, example, 71
Side hustle, importance/
        acceptance, 119–120
Skills, transfer, 63
SMART method, usage, 104
Soft skills, impact, 3
Soul searching, 74
Sounding board, 74
Special light, need, 7–8
Spencer, Eric, 136
Staffing firms, hiring, 50
Story
    creation, 27
    refinement/adjustment, 30
    writing, 19
Storytelling
    comfort, 23
    effectiveness, 20
    goal, 30
    self-recording, 29
Strength/resilience,
        development, 26
StrengthsFinder 2.0, usage,
        42
Stress, 127–128
    impact, 122
    reduction, 123

Success, 101, 167
   appearance, defining, 114
   finding, 22
   framework, 113, 115–116,
      175–180

T
Tails That Teach (charity), 79
Target list
   completion, 68
   creation, 62–63
   organizations, 71–72
Team
   delegation, consideration, 58
   "filling in the blanks," 116
   goals, 116–118, 178–180
   involvement, 109
   meeting, 45
Timeout, usage, 122
Toolbox, building, 31
Truth, stretching
      (avoidance), 23

U
Unconditional love, life
      lessons, 79
Uniqueness, 14–15, 140–141

V
Value proposition,
      identification,
      115, 174–175

van der Meer, Audrey, 13
Vesely, Ruby, 136
Video meeting, login, 87
Vision, 121
   writing, 113

W
Williamson, Marianne, 84
Work
   attention, 134
   changes, 3
   enjoyment, 12
   joy, finding, 135
   requirement, 7–8
   rules, 42
   stress, 87
   understanding, 4
Workforce, exit, 36
Work in progress, 83–84

Y
*You, Me, We: Why We All
      Need a Friend at Work
      (and How to Show
      Up as One)* (Barrett/
      Spencer/Vesely),
      136

Z
Ziglar, Zig, 134
Zuckerberg, Mark, 28

Life is better when you're doing what you love!

Let's shine a light on your passions and discover your purpose.

✧

Wherever you are in your career journey there's no better time than now to design your best work life.

Visit MaryOlsonMenzel.com for help throughout your career journey with:

- Articles
- Resources and Tools
- Podcasts
- Workshops
- and more...

MaryOlsonMenzel.com